SPOOKY
Virginia

Also in the Spooky Series by S. E. Schlosser and Paul G. Hoffman:

Spooky California
Spooky Campfire Tales
Spooky Canada
Spooky Christmas
Spooky Colorado
Spooky Florida
Spooky Georgia
Spooky Great Smokies
Spooky Indiana
Spooky Maryland
Spooky Massachusetts
Spooky Michigan
Spooky Montana
Spooky New England
Spooky New Jersey
Spooky New Orleans
Spooky New York
Spooky North Carolina
Spooky Ohio
Spooky Oregon
Spooky Pennsylvania
Spooky South
Spooky Southwest
Spooky Texas
Spooky Virginia
Spooky Washington
Spooky Wisconsin
Spooky Yellowstone

SPOOKY
Virginia

Tales of Hauntings, Strange Happenings,
and Other Local Lore

SECOND EDITION

RETOLD BY S. E. SCHLOSSER
ILLUSTRATED BY PAUL G. HOFFMAN

Globe
Pequot
ESSEX, CONNECTICUT

Globe
Pequot

An imprint of Globe Pequot, the trade division of
The Rowman & Littlefield Publishing Group, Inc.
4501 Forbes Blvd., Ste. 200
Lanham, MD 20706
www.rowman.com

Distributed by NATIONAL BOOK NETWORK

British Library Cataloguing in Publication Information available

Library of Congress Cataloging-in-Publication Data
Names: Schlosser, S. E., author. | Hoffman, Paul G.
Title: Spooky Virginia: tales of hauntings, strange happenings, and other
    local lore / retold by S. E. Schlosser; illustrated by Paul G. Hoffman.
Description: Second edition. | Essex, Connecticut: Globe Pequot, 2023. |
    Series: Spooky | Includes index.
Identifiers: LCCN 2023001191 (print) | LCCN 2023001192 (ebook) |
    ISBN 9781493069866 (paperback) | ISBN 9781493069873 (epub)
Subjects: LCSH: Ghosts—Virginia. | Haunted places—Virginia.
Classification: LCC BF1472.U6 S336 2023 (print) | LCC BF1472.U6
    (ebook) | DDC 133.109755—dc23/eng/20230203
LC record available at https://lccn.loc.gov/2023001191
LC ebook record available at https://lccn.loc.gov/2023001192

*For my family: David, Dena, Tim, Arlene, Hannah,
Seth, Theo, Emma, Nathan, Ben, Deb, Gabe, Clare,
Jack, Chris, Karen, Davey, and Aunt Mil.*

*For the Mertz family: Vince, Kristen, Seth,
Hannah, Theo, Sarah, and Kevin Silva.*

*For Erin Turner, Paul Hoffman, David Legere, and all the
wonderful folks at Globe Pequot Press, with my thanks.*

*For Aunt Liz, Uncle Rich, and Steven; for Davy and Tammy;
and for Dan, Kirsten, and Anne. Thanks for your hospitality.*

Contents

MAP   x

INTRODUCTION   xiii

PART ONE: GHOST STORIES

1.   *Goggle-Eyed Jim*   2
     GREAT DISMAL SWAMP

2.   *The Convert*   9
     COEBURN

3.   *The Finger Bone*   16
     LEE COUNTY

4.   *Shep*   26
     SHENANDOAH VALLEY

5.   *Old House Woods*   33
     MATHEWS COUNTY

6.   *A Love Betrayed*   41
     WILLIAMSBURG

7.   *I Will Find Her*   47
     LAKE DRUMMOND, GREAT DISMAL SWAMP

8.   *Elbow Road*   52
     VIRGINIA BEACH

9.   *Shower of Stones*   60
     NEWPORT

10. *Elopement*   68
     RICHMOND

11. *Angel*   78
     FREDERICKSBURG

Contents

12. *The Horseman*   87
    BOWLING GREEN

13. *Phantasie*   97
    JAMESTOWN

14. *Old 97*   105
    DANVILLE

15. *Bunny Man Bridge*   111
    CLIFTON

16. *Hold Him, Tabb*   116
    HAMPTON, VIRGINIA

17. *The Haunted Tower*   121
    PITTSYLVANIA

18. *Handprints*   129
    YORKTOWN

PART TWO: POWERS OF DARKNESS AND LIGHT

19. *River Witch*   140
    FARMVILLE

20. *The Witch's Shoulder*   146
    BIG LAUREL, WISE COUNTY

21. *The Fiddler and the Wolves*   153
    GRAYSON COUNTY

22. *The White Dove*   159
    DANVILLE

23. *The Black Dog*   167
    BEDFORD COUNTY

24. *Jack Ma Lantern*   176
    FRONT ROYAL

25. *Kitty*   185
    SMYTH COUNTY

Contents

26. *Fire!*   192
    RICHMOND

27. *Foul Smell*   200
    ALEXANDRIA

28. *Trail of Blood*   205
    GLOUCESTER

29. *Rupp*   214
    BIG STONE GAP

30. *The Lady*   225
    RICHMOND

31. *Devil in the Flour Barrel*   232
    AMHERST COUNTY

32. *Consecration*   239
    MOUNT VERNON

33. *The Honest Wine Merchant*   246
    RICHMOND

34. *The Seventh Window*   252
    CHARLOTTESVILLE

RESOURCES   265

ABOUT THE AUTHOR   269

ABOUT THE ILLUSTRATOR   269

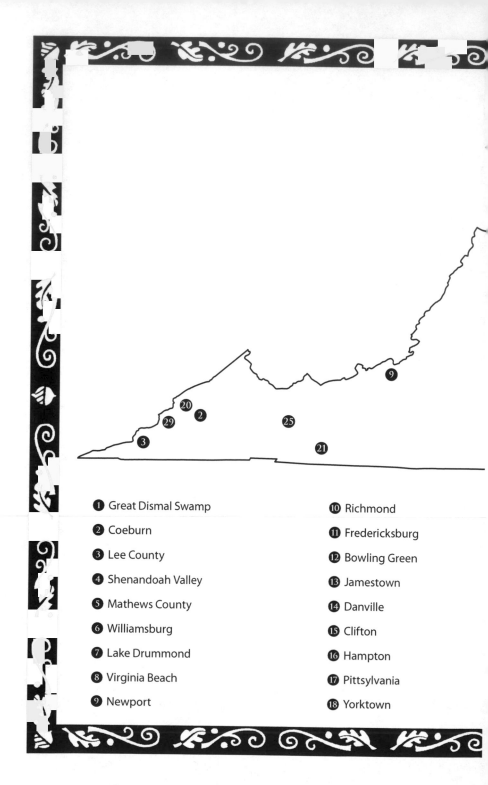

1 Great Dismal Swamp
2 Coeburn
3 Lee County
4 Shenandoah Valley
5 Mathews County
6 Williamsburg
7 Lake Drummond
8 Virginia Beach
9 Newport

10 Richmond
11 Fredericksburg
12 Bowling Green
13 Jamestown
14 Danville
15 Clifton
16 Hampton
17 Pittsylvania
18 Yorktown

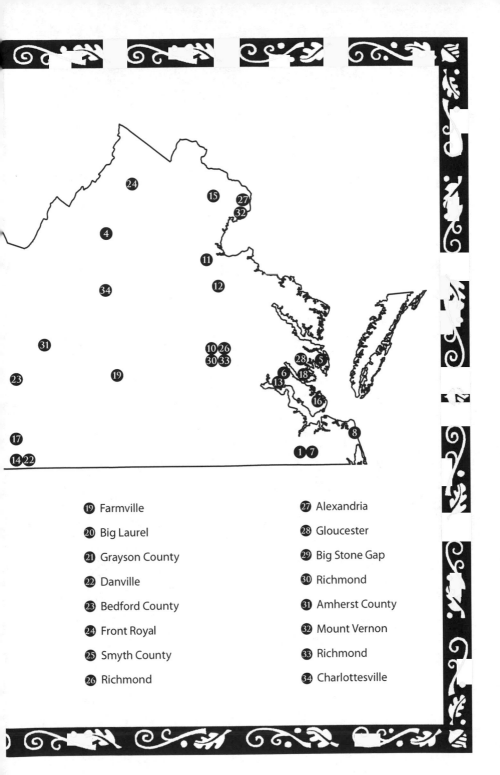

19 Farmville

20 Big Laurel

21 Grayson County

22 Danville

23 Bedford County

24 Front Royal

25 Smyth County

26 Richmond

27 Alexandria

28 Gloucester

29 Big Stone Gap

30 Richmond

31 Amherst County

32 Mount Vernon

33 Richmond

34 Charlottesville

Introduction

It was the last day of my Spooky Virginia research trip, so I got up early. I wanted to sneak in a visit to the Cape Henry lighthouses before my journey took me to the Eastern Shore of Virginia and Chincoteague Island. The day was sunny and warm, and I passed through the Fort Story checkout point with no trouble. A few minutes later I was grinning broadly as not one but two lighthouses came into view.

I pulled into the parking lot, my eyes fixed on the black-and-white wonder to my right. The new Cape Henry Lighthouse was still in use and was lovely to behold. As I walked toward the lighthouse, I spotted an osprey overhead carrying a fish in his talons. I took a few quick photos of its flight and then turned my camera to the lighthouse. After photographing the new light, I headed across the street to the old Cape Henry Lighthouse—made of red brick—where I chatted with the people in the little store before climbing up and up to the top to admire the view. Standing on top of the lighthouse in Virginia Beach on a warm sunny morning, it was hard to picture what it must have been like for the young couple who saw the ghost of murdered Mrs. Woble one night while driving along another Virginia Beach road not far from where I stood (*Elbow Road*).

Mrs. Woble is not the only ghost to haunt the Chesapeake Bay region. Over in Mathews County, *Old House Woods* is haunted by a plethora of spirits, including seventeenth-century soldiers guarding buried treasure. And in Gloucester, a *Trail of*

Blood will sometimes appear during the first snowfall, leading to the cemetery where a young woman was once buried alive.

And these stories are just the tip of the iceberg. During my Virginia wanderings I came across wonderfully creepy tales like the story of *Rupp*, a vampire who plagued Big Stone Gap in the nineteenth century. In Bedford County is told the legend of a *Black Dog* that haunted a mountaintop road, guarding the body of its slain master. In Lee County, a ghost once led a preacher to her murderer using her *Finger Bone*. In the Great Dismal Swamp, *Goggle-Eyed Jim* kept stealing horses long after he was dead. In Danville the whistle from the *Old 97* still blows around 2:00 p.m. over the ravine where the wildcat train was wrecked, and *The White Dove* still flies in and out of a haunted house.

Virginia's spooky folklore has many different faces. On the one hand are humorous stories like the *Devil in the Flour Barrel* and on the other, heart-wrenching tales like *The Horseman*, in which the sound of a phantom horseman heralded the death of each of a Bowling Green couple's five sons. There is the sublime legend of the *Consecration* of George Washington and the hair-raising urban legends of *Bunny Man Bridge* and *Foul Smell*. In the swamplands near Front Royal, the hissing *Jack Ma Lantern* lures travelers to their doom, and in the Shenandoah Valley, a dog returns from the grave to lead his master to safety after a flood wrecks the bridge (*Shep*).

Virginia's landscape is as beautiful and as varied as its folklore. I loved the special time spent exploring my home state. After many wanderings and much digging through dusty archives, I have compiled my favorite spooky tales to share with you. Enjoy!

—Sandy Schlosser

PART ONE
Ghost Stories

1

Goggle-Eyed Jim

GREAT DISMAL SWAMP

He was a notorious scoundrel and a horse thief. *And* he was the bane of my existence. Goggle-Eyed Jim they called him. The things they called me when I failed to catch him . . . Well, that's beside the point.

Being the only lawman in a backcountry area close to the Great Dismal Swamp ain't easy. Too many of my suspects lost themselves in the trees and undergrowth of the swamp, leaving me behind in mud up to my armpits and with—more often than not—a lump on my head where I hit it on a low-hanging branch. It was infuriating.

But Goggle-Eyed Jim was the worst. Week after week, angry citizens would storm into my office demanding justice. Their reports were always the same. They'd been awakened by the clanging of a cowbell and a huge hullabaloo out in the barn. By the time they'd grabbed a rifle and run outside, a dark-cloaked figure with huge goggles that reflected oddly in the moonlight would flash by on the back of the citizen's best horse, laughing as he went. Goggle-Eyed Jim had a hee-haw of a laugh, like a braying donkey. But he was no laughing matter.

GOGGLE-EYED JIM

When the mayor brought home a real beaut of a stallion that October, I set up a trap for Goggle-Eyed Jim. I arranged with the mayor to sleep in his barn in the hayloft overlooking the horse stalls every night for a week. We were both sure that Goggle-Eyed Jim would come for the horse as soon as he heard about it. And the mayor made sure to parade his new purchase up and down the streets of our little town, boasting all the while of his prowess as a race horse, his beauty, his price.

Sure enough, three days later I was awakened from a strangely deep sleep by the clanging of a cowbell. I cursed and rolled over in my prickly bed of hay, throwing off my old horse blanket and reaching for my rifle. The blanket sent up a huge cloud of dust, and I sneezed as I snatched up the gun and scrambled on hands and knees to the edge of the loft. How had Goggle-Eyed Jim gotten into the barn without my hearing him? I am the lightest of sleepers, but not even the soft whicker of a horse had disturbed my slumber, though I'd been awakened by much smaller sounds on previous evenings.

As I reached the edge of the loft, I saw a horse's tail swishing through the open barn door. By now the other horses were neighing and whinnying to beat the band. Many of them reared when I made a foolish leap directly down to the floor from my perch, still clutching my rifle. I could have busted a leg but somehow made it with only a painful twist to my ankle. I rushed outside, stopping right beside the barn door to take aim at the fleeing rider with his flapping black cloak and reflecting goggle eyes. The mayor came rushing out of the house as I took my first shot, and he got off a second shot as I reloaded and aimed again.

I was sure I'd hit the scalawag with my first shot, and I know I nailed him with the second. But he kept on riding down the lane and out of sight, and the air was filled with the hee-haw of his laughter as he got away again!

The mayor was not pleased. Folks started talking about running me out of town—or hauling out the tar and feathers. I was about ready to resign when I got a real lead at last on the elusive horse thief. A fella who lived deep in the Great Dismal saw Goggle-Eyed Jim hanging out at a rickety old cabin near Lake Drummond that was once used as a hideout by pirates. As soon as he described the place, I knew exactly where he meant. I loaded up my guns and headed into the swamp in the golden afternoon light. It took a couple of hours to locate the old cabin and another couple minutes to find myself a hiding place.

Darkness fell quickly, and no Goggle-Eyed Jim. I made myself comfortable. I didn't care how long I had to wait. I'd wait until kingdom come if I had to. That darned horse thief was going to jail, and I was the one who was going to put him there.

Well, I thought I'd kept my eyes and ears open, but I must have dozed off, 'cause suddenly there was a light shining in the upstairs window and I could hear voices coming from the cabin. One of them was a woman's voice, and she was giggling and cooing like a dove. Seems like I'd caught Goggle-Eyed Jim in a tryst. Too bad for him.

I hauled out an old ladder I'd spotted in the lean-to on the side of the cabin and put it against the wall. Cradling my pistol, I climbed up the ladder and peered into the window. Yep. There he was: Goggle-Eyed Jim. He was swathed in his long black cloak and still wearing his green goggles. They seemed to glow in the lantern light—made my skin crawl. I'd be glad to see the creepy fellow behind bars.

At that moment, a lady wearing not much to speak of flounced into the room with a bottle of brandy and a couple of tin cups. She cozied up to Goggle-Eyed Jim, cooing something flirtatious into his ear.

"Right-o. Your time is up, old chap," I muttered, pulling out my pistol. The bounty on Goggle-Eyed Jim said "dead or alive," and I didn't much care which it was at that moment. He'd made my life too miserable for too long for me to feel any compassion for him.

As if he sensed my thoughts, Goggle-Eyed Jim turned his face toward the window where I crouched atop the ladder. His eyes, behind the goggles, seemed to glow with a greenish-blue light. His face was so gray and withered, he looked like a corpse. He grinned suddenly, showing a mouth with more gap than yellow teeth. I aimed and fired. I hit him too. The woman shrieked and fled, and Goggle-Eyed Jim clamped a hand over his chest and staggered dramatically toward the far window. By the time I clambered inside the cabin, he was poised on the window ledge. He gave me a jaunty wave and then tumbled out the window, still dramatically clutching his chest.

I tore down the stairs, rushing past the floozy and out into the tall grass of the yard. A figure in a dark cloak lay in the grass, his green goggles glowing in the moonlight.

"I gotcha!" I shouted, racing toward him. And then I stopped abruptly with a gasp of fear. The prone figure before me began floating upward from his grassy bed, his arms still outstretched. Goggle-Eyed Jim was . . . well, he was glowing from within! And, I realized with an ice-cold shudder, I could see the weedy lawn right through his body. He was a ghost!

By this time, Goggle-Eyed Jim was floating about six feet in the air, his body still sprawled flat on nothing. Suddenly he sat bolt upright and snorted: "Hee-Haw! Hee-Haw!"

I staggered backward with a gasp of disbelief as the ghastly figure started to spin around and around, faster and faster, still snorting with laughter. A dark hole appeared behind the glowing figure with its piercing green goggles, which were the only part of the spirit I could make out in the furious, body-blurring twirl. Suddenly the spinning figure fell backward into the dark hole, which shut with a loud snap. The empty yard was filled with the smell of sulfur.

I let out a shriek of pure, gut-wrenching terror and went crashing away into the woods. Behind me, the floozy let out an equally loud shriek and went crashing off in the other direction. I'd run only about a hundred steps before I broke through a tangle of bushes into a hidden meadow and was nearly trampled by the mayor's stallion, which had been happily grazing in the moonlight until I came crashing along.

The stallion wasn't the only horse in the meadow. There were at least six more horses, all of them reported stolen by Goggle-Eyed Jim. I stared at the horses in wonder. Just how long had Goggle-Eyed Jim been a ghost?

Casting my mind back over the reported thefts and matching them up to the horses before me, I reckoned that the horse thief had been dead at least six months. Not that this small detail had fazed Goggle-Eyed Jim. He'd just kept right on stealing horses, though he had no need to sell them now. No wonder bullets didn't affect him! I *knew* both my shots had landed that night at the mayor's house.

Standing there in that moonlit meadow, my skin still crawling from my encounter with the ghost, I wondered how I was going to explain the situation to the mayor. Then I shrugged, mounted the stallion bareback, and rode home. I'd return for the other horses in the morning.

The mayor was mighty glad to get his horse back, though he wasn't terribly convinced by my story about the ghostly Goggle-Eyed Jim. Still, once he'd seen all them horses grazing in the hidden meadow, he decided at least part of my story must be true. Anyhow, he okayed my plan to have a priest out to the old cabin to do an exorcism. And that did the trick. Goggle-Eyed Jim's days of horse thieving were over. And I got to keep my job. So one of us had a happy ending. I'm glad it was me!

2

The Convert

COEBURN

Old Man Greer was just about the grumpiest fellow in the South. And he was an atheist to boot. His wife tried and tried to get him to go to church. *She* said he should set a good example to his son and daughters. *He* said he wasn't gonna be a hypocrite like the fellows who got drunk in the local tavern every weekday and then sat in the front pew on Sunday. And that was that.

Missus Greer was a game lady. Year after year she kept on trying. Every Christmas and Easter, she'd invite her man to church, and every Christmas and Easter he'd say "No thank you" and go out hunting or fishing instead.

"Papa ought to go to church," her little son, Timmy, said to his Mama. "I'd like him to hear me sing."

"I'd like that too," Missus Greer said with a sigh. Timmy had a lovely soprano voice and was a soloist in their community church. But even on Sundays when Timmy sang a solo, Old Man Greer wouldn't go to church.

Sour though he was on religion, Old Man Greer was proud of his children, and he supported their academics and their hobbies. So whenever Timmy had a solo at church, his father

THE CONVERT

had the boy perform again for the family when they got home from the service.

It was shortly after Timmy performed "Amazing Grace" in church that he fell sick with pneumonia. The doctor did everything in his power to save the child, but Timmy died within a week. Old Man Greer was devastated by the loss of his child. In the long weeks and months that followed, he clung all the tighter to his two remaining children and begrudged all the time the girls spent in church with their mama. "If you'd come to church with us, you wouldn't be parted from us so much," his youngest daughter said to him. But Old Man Greer still wouldn't go to church.

In the springtime following Timmy's death, a revival preacher came to town. The minister of the local church scheduled tent meetings every night for a whole week, and everyone in town planned to go. Everyone but Old Man Greer.

"Nonsense," he grumbled to his wife. "You should stay at home with me."

But Missus Greer was a spirited as well as spiritual lady. If she wanted to go to the revival meetings, she was going to go to the revival meetings *and* take the girls with her. And so they went. The preacher was an eloquent speaker, and the girls delighted in the wonderful music and the moving sermon. They talked about it so much when they got home that Old Man Greer went out to the barn to avoid hearing them.

Missus Greer, who was determined to save her husband's soul, followed him to the barn and begged him to come with them the next evening, but he said "no" real firm. He started mucking out the horse stall for emphasis, which sent his wife scurrying back to the house so she wouldn't soil her dress. But

Missus Greer wasn't done with her husband. She asked the minister to go to her husband's place of business the next day to invite him personally to the tent meeting. The minister went. Old Man Greer was polite to the minister—almost—but he made it clear that he didn't hold with church and wasn't going to a revival meeting. Ever.

Then fate took a hand.

When Missus Greer and the girls got home from the tent meeting on the third day of the revival, they found Old Man Greer standing in front of the house, staring up the hill at the family graveyard.

"What's wrong, Papa?" asked his oldest girl, slipping her hand through his arm. He patted her hand fondly but didn't take his eyes off the graveyard.

"I thought I heard Ti . . . someone singing," he said gruffly.

The color drained out of Missus Greer's cheeks. She missed her only son horribly, and this reminder of her loss left her speechless. The four Greers clung to one another for a moment, staring up at the graveyard in the dim light of the moon. Then they went inside.

No sooner had the door closed behind them than the singing began. The voice was a pure soprano; the tune, "Amazing Grace." It was the voice of Timmy Greer. Missus Greer swayed alarmingly, and her husband rushed forward to catch her before she fell. He sat her gently down in her rocking chair, all the while listening as the singing voice came closer and closer to the house. Abruptly the voice ceased; a glowing light eased itself through the wall in the upper corner of the room, right by the ceiling. The four Greers stared at the light in terrified amazement. Old Man Greer was all over goose bumps, and his hands shook as he rubbed his wife's shoulders to comfort her.

Slowly the light moved across the ceiling and into the Greers' bedroom. Old Man Greer followed it, and his wife and girls followed him. They peered in the door of the darkened room and saw the light crawl down the wall and disappear underneath the bed.

"Papa?" quavered the younger daughter. "Wh . . . what is it?"

"I don't know," said Old Man Greer grimly. He went reluctantly over to the bed and looked underneath it, but there was nothing there. Missus Greer gave a sigh of relief and sagged a little against the doorjamb. Then she gasped, and the girls with her, as the light reappeared just above the bed and went crawling back up the wall. Old Man Greer scrambled out from under the bed and watched with them as the light went back into the front parlor and out through the front wall. And then they all heard a high, boy-soprano voice singing the second verse of "Amazing Grace." The voice headed off in the direction of the graveyard, growing fainter and fainter until it disappeared.

The whole family was shaken by the incident, and Old Man Greer had difficulty sleeping that night. But he still refused to go to the revival meeting the next evening. "But, Papa, you heard Ti . . . you heard the voice last night," his elder girl protested. "I'm sure it was a sign."

"Hush, my girl. You know my mind on the matter," Old Man Greer said.

Missus Greer shook her head to shush the girl, and the womenfolk headed out to the tent meeting. It was another fantastic service, but Missus Greer had difficulty keeping her mind on the sermon. She hurried the girls home afterward instead of staying to socialize with their friends.

Things were nice and normal when they got home, and the whole family got to bed early that evening. Old Man Greer was fast asleep when the singing began up in the graveyard. "Amazing Grace, how sweet the sound," the voice sang sweetly as it approached the house. Old Man Greer and his wife sat bolt upright in bed as the song ceased just outside the house. The ghost light entered through the front parlor wall, crawled rapidly across the parlor ceiling and into their bedroom, and within moments had disappeared beneath their bed. As soon as the light vanished, the bed began to rock and dance its way across the floor. Missus Greer screamed, and Old Man Greer picked her up and tumbled them both out of the bed. Missus Greer kept screaming as her daughters raced into the room. The women watched in amazement as Old Man Greer wrestled with the bed, trying to make it stop moving about. But he kept falling on his face or tumbling onto his rear end until Missus Greer told him to stop.

The four Greers stood by the door and watched the bed's antics for several long minutes before the recalcitrant piece of furniture walked itself back to its place by the wall. The ghost light reappeared, tracing its way up and out of the house. A moment later a voice began singing "Amazing Grace" out in the yard, getting fainter as it made its way up toward the graveyard.

Word swiftly got around town about the Greers' dancing bed. After the revival meeting the next evening, practically everybody in town came to the Greers' place to have a look. They weren't disappointed. Right on schedule, the voice came singing its way to the house, the light slipped into the Greers'

bedroom and disappeared under the bed, and the bed began to dance. Four strong men took hold of its corners, but the bed shook them off and jiggled around and around the room. Even after the bed went back to its corner, the light crawled away, and the voice went back to the graveyard, folks stuck around, hoping for a repeat performance.

Old Man Greer had dark rings around his eyes the next day, and he didn't speak much at work. When he got home, he shaved carefully, put on his best suit, and, to the complete astonishment of his wife and daughters, escorted his womenfolk to the tent meeting. He didn't sing, but he seemed to be listening when the preacher spoke. He escorted his family home in silence, raising his voice only when he found that some of his neighbors wanted to spend the night at his house to see the dancing bed. He sent them on their way lickety-split with their ears burning. He seemed resigned to the arrival of the voice, light, and dancing bed. He just picked up his wife and carried her into the parlor to wait until the bed stopped jiggling and they could get some sleep.

Old Man Greer held out for two more nights. On the third, he went up for the altar call and got religion at last, much to the delight of his wife and daughters.

From that moment, the haunting ceased. The light and the voice were never seen or heard again.

3

The Finger Bone

LEE COUNTY

As a preacher, I've seen some strange things during my years of ministry. But the one that stands out most in my mind is the incident of the finger bone. I was traveling through Lee County with two friends—a lawyer and a doctor, both of whom lived in my hometown—when night caught us out on the road. Seeing a tiny cabin nearby, we rode our weary horses down the lane to inquire of the owner if there was a barn or a vacant house where we could camp for the night.

"Well, preacher," the man said after I'd introduced myself and made my request, "there's a vacant house not far from here. But you don't want to stay there on account of the ghost!"

A ghost, I thought with a spark of interest.

"Spirits don't frighten me," I told the man, patting the Bible I always kept in a travel bag at my side. "Where's this house?"

After some hesitation, the man gave us directions to the house and loaded us up with wood for a fire. Then he bade us a fearful farewell, running back into his house as though the devil were on his heels. We all heard the door slam behind him. The unspoken message was very clear: If we wanted to mess with ghosts, that was our business. He'd warned us, and that was as

THE FINGER BONE

much as he was going to do for fools that knowingly stayed in a haunted house.

The vacant house was not far away from the man's cabin. Standing in a tall grove of pines, it had been neglected for so long that part of the roof had fallen in and only half of the porch was still attached to the house. Most of the windows were shattered, and vines grew everywhere. It was a dismal sight in the light of the small lantern my lawyer friend produced from his saddlebag.

We rubbed the horses down and hobbled them in the shelter of the huge pines. It was a grassy place beside a very small spring and would have been a pleasant place if it weren't for the menacing structure beside it. We walked up onto the wobbling front porch, and I pulled open the front door, which gave a sinister squeal as it swung forward.

"Nasty atmosphere," my doctor friend observed as we stepped into the decrepit front hall. "No wonder folks think this place is haunted."

We stared in dismay at the tattered, mud-stained wallpaper and the mildewed carpet on the floor. It must have been an elegant home, once. I could see several moldering portraits and silver candle sconces affixed to the walls, but these were so tarnished they barely reflected the lantern light. Dusty cobwebs festooned the ceiling, and a small tree was growing halfway up the center staircase.

The air in the house was many degrees cooler than outside. I shivered, feeling invisible eyes peering at me from somewhere close. The gaze didn't feel particularly menacing, but the sense of otherworldliness made my skin crawl. I knew in that instant that the stories were correct. This place was haunted.

"There's still a roof over this room," the lawyer called from the front parlor. "And I think we can get a fire lit in that grate."

"Excellent," said the doctor, hurrying into the room with a shudder. "For some reason, I feel terribly chilled."

I clutched the travel bag with my Bible inside and went to join my friends. We soon had a fire crackling in the fireplace and a tin of baked beans bubbling over the coals beside a couple of roasting potatoes. The delicious smell filled the air, driving away thoughts of ghosts. As we ate our late supper, we discussed the house and its ghost story.

"I don't believe in ghosts," said the lawyer, shaking his head.

"There is at least one tale of a ghost in the Holy Bible," I told him, wiping my mouth on a napkin extracted from the doctor's saddlebag. "I do believe in ghosts. And I think this place is haunted."

"What would you do if you saw a ghost?" asked the doctor with interest.

"Speak to it of course," I said with more aplomb then I felt. "If a spirit shows up tonight, you boys best leave the talking to me."

"You can bet on it," said the doctor. "I'll be too busy running to talk!"

That made us laugh. We were in good spirits as we spread blankets out on the dusty floor and lay down to sleep. But sleep eluded me. The wind was soughing through the tops of the pine trees, and the air in the parlor was growing more and more frigid, though it was midsummer. Chills crept up my arms and legs, and a feeling of dread kept me still and silent under my blanket. Something was coming. I could sense it long before the noises began.

The first manifestation came from the loft overhead. There was a deep sighing sound, followed by footsteps and the clanking of heavy chains being dragged across the floor. The doctor rolled over and his head fell off the saddlebag that he was using as a pillow. On the far side of the fire, the lawyer sat bolt upright, staring overhead. Both men turned frightened faces toward me in the dim light of the dying fire as the door to the hallway banged open and a chill breeze swept through the room.

"R . . . remember. Let me do the talking," I stammered, trying to sound brave. My whole body was shaking so badly, I couldn't have run even if I'd wanted to. Inside my head I kept repeating, "I am a man of God. Nothing can harm me." I only wished I believed it.

We heard the chains dragging down the staircase and saw a bluish light fill the hallway outside. Then the glowing figure of a woman appeared in the doorway. The bluish light from her body illuminated the front parlor and cast strange, swirling shadows into the corners. Wrapped in heavy chains, she moaned softly as she made her way past the cowering lawyer, whose teeth were chattering so loud I could hear them from across the room. The glowing woman stopped in front of the fireplace and turned to face us, her face twisted in agony, her hands wringing together so hard that phantom blood spurted through her translucent fingers.

This was my big moment—and I nearly flubbed it. I had to clear my throat twice before any sound would emerge.

"In the name of the Father and the Son and the Holy Ghost, what do you want?" I intoned, sounding like a schoolboy playing a game rather than a minister of the Lord declaiming to a phantom. I had been taught to recite this litany three times in order to release the voice of the spirit, and by the third time I sounded almost myself again.

At the third repetition of my question, the ghost began to moan again, a sound that raised every hair on my body and made my legs quiver as though they wanted to run. It was sheer willpower that kept me seated. The doctor gasped and ducked his head under his blanket as the moan grew louder and higher in pitch. The lawyer clapped his hands to his ears as the piercing sound hit an unbearably high note. Then it ceased, and the phantom spoke.

"I was murdered in this house," she whispered. "My sweetheart killed me for my money and buried me in the cellar. I want you to find my bones. Fiiind myyy boooones!"

The ghost's last three words became another high-pitched wailing. I hugged my Bible against my chest, wondering if I should adjure the spirit again in the name of Father, Son, and Holy Spirit. But her wailing stopped abruptly and she continued to speak.

"When you find my bones, you must give them a Christian burial. All save the bone of my little finger. I want you to keep the finger bone, and I want you to set a dinner and invite all your neighbors. After you have asked the blessing, pass the finger bone around on a silver plate. The bone will stick to the hand of the man who killed me."

The ghost paused again and moaned. This time, her voice went low and deep. It rumbled in the pit of my stomach, making me nauseous. Across the room, the lawyer curled up into a little ball, rocking back and forth with his hands still clamped over his ears. I fumbled in my shirt and pulled out a silver cross on a chain, which I held up to the spirit. The sight of the cross recalled her to herself, and the sound abruptly ceased.

"Before my sweetheart killed me, I hid my money where he could not find it. If you carry out my request, I will reveal the hiding place to you, and you may have the money with my blessing," the phantom concluded.

She stared deep into my eyes, her glowing orbs burning into mine. I swallowed three times and stammered, "I will do as you ask."

Satisfied, the ghost vanished with a small puff of air; the room went dark, save for the glowing embers of the fire. The doctor groaned and poked an eye out from under the blanket. "Is it safe to come out?" he whispered hoarsely.

"I . . . I think so," I muttered.

Across the room, the lawyer groaned almost as piteously as the phantom. "There are times," he said, "when I wish grown men were allowed to run home screaming for their mothers."

"You and me both," I said sincerely.

We waited until the next morning when the sun was shining brightly over the pine grove before we went down into the cellar and disinterred the murdered girl. Then we took the bones to the local sheriff and told him where we'd found the body. We all attended the funeral of the unknown girl a few days later. The only bone missing when the coffin was placed into the ground was the bone of her little finger.

As the ghost requested, I threw a big dinner party a week after the funeral and invited the whole neighborhood. I found it a little strange that she wanted me to invite the people from my town, which was many miles from where her body had been buried. But I obeyed her request to the letter. After the blessing,

I passed around the bone on a silver platter, calling it a curiosity and asking my neighbors to guess what it was.

The woman seated beside me at the table gave me an odd look, but she picked up the bone as requested and examined it.

"Is it some kind of animal bone?" she asked.

"Not a bad guess," I replied. "Let's see what others think."

She put the bone back on the silver platter and handed it to the lawyer, who winked at me, picked up the bone, and pretended to examine it. "I think it comes from a raccoon," he said before putting the bone back on the platter and handing it to the man seated beside him. The man was the cousin of one of my parishioners, who was boarding at the home of his relative.

As soon as the man picked up the finger bone, I knew he was the one.

"I'm not sure if it is an animal bone," he said and then tried to turn it over. But the bone stuck to his fingers and wouldn't come off. "What's this?" he exclaimed, trying and failing to drop the bone. He shook his hand violently, but the bone was stuck fast.

My eyes met those of the sheriff from Lee County, who had been invited to join the dinner party.

"You are correct," I said loudly over the man's alarmed exclamations. "It is not the bone of an animal. It is the bone of a murdered woman found in a house over in Lee County."

The man's eyes widened in sudden understanding and color flooded his face. "Get it off me," he begged, holding his hand out toward me. "Get it off!"

"It is not in my power to remove the finger bone," I said softly. "Only you can remove it."

The other guests looked from the bone to the man's face to me, puzzled. Then one or two blinked in horror as understanding dawned. If it was the bone of a murdered woman and it was sticking to this man's hands, did that mean he was . . .?

I saw the internal struggle reflected in the man's expression. He realized that he was caught but was not sure whether to confess or run. He went very pale and slowly slumped against the back of the chair, staring at the bone stuck to his hand. Then he jerked to his feet, and screamed, "I did it! I confess! I killed my sweetheart for her money and buried her in the cellar!"

As he spoke, the bone quivered on his hand. Every eye was fixed upon it as it slowly fell from the man's hand, clattering down onto the silver platter that sat demurely on the table in front of him. Then the sheriff came quietly around the table and led the shaking man away.

When my house was empty again save for my two friends, I asked if they wanted a share of the treasure, should the ghost keep her promise. They both shook their heads. They were well-to-do and had everything they wanted, whereas I was a poor minister who could barely make ends meet.

"If you find it, you keep it," said my lawyer friend, and the doctor agreed.

The ghost did appear to me later that night and told me exactly where to find the money she'd hidden from her sweetheart. I went to the location the next day, and the money was right where she said it would be. It amounted to several thousand dollars—enough to keep me in comfort the rest of my days. In fact, I used it to buy and restore the haunted house in the pine grove.

In due time I brought a bride home to that house, and together we raised a family there. It became a very happy place indeed, filled with love and laughter and frequent visits from my doctor and lawyer friends. But the ghost girl was never seen again.

4

Shep

SHENANDOAH VALLEY

It was full night when the train let me off at the station, but I didn't care. There was no one to meet me there either, and I still didn't care. They'd have been there if they had known I was coming. But I wanted to surprise my folks, so I hadn't telephoned ahead. The station was several miles from my home, which meant a longish walk on a dark night. But that didn't bother me. After surviving the beaches of Normandy, what was a walk of a couple miles, even in the dark? No one was shooting at me; no one was cursing my very existence; no one wanted me dead at any cost. It was bliss. *And* my family was at the other end of the walk. What more could a soldier ask for?

I slung my kit over my shoulder and started marching down the dirt road by the river. Lots of mud got on my boots. There must have been some spring storms around here lately. But I didn't care about the mud. My thoughts were full of home. I couldn't wait to see Mama's face when I walked in the door. She'd be so surprised! And Daddy would be so choked up he wouldn't say a word for ten minutes for fear he'd start bawling like a baby. I could picture it all so clearly. The road was dark, and the trees on either side rustled in the wind. There wasn't

SHEP

much of a moon that night, but it didn't matter. I'd been walking this roadway all my life, and my feet knew the way home. The river was chattering and swirling in its banks—running real fast. Spring floods, I thought. There must have been quite a wash here not too long ago. Still, the voice of the river was company during this final leg of my journey home.

I'd have to make a turn soon and take the bridge over the river. It should be coming up any minute. Straining my eyes in the darkness, I made out a dark span across the water a little closer than I remembered. As I approached, I realized why. A second, girder bridge—the one I had been crossing all my life—lay beyond the one I'd seen first. So, they'd built a new bridge. I supposed it was time. The girder bridge was getting old and worn out after many years of use.

I fancied trying out the new bridge. It would be a new experience, plus it was closer and would get me home quicker. The notion of getting home quicker brought a smile to my lips. *I'm coming, Mama!*

I was only a few yards from the new bridge when a shaggy bullet of pure animal energy raced toward me and leapt against my chest. I staggered backward, my arms full of dog.

"Shep!" I shouted. "Oh, Shep!"

Tough soldier that I was, I nearly broke into tears as our family dog danced around me. Shep threw himself again and again into my arms, only to wiggle free when sheer delight forced him to twirl in circles, chasing his tail. Finally I caught him close, wrapped both my arms around his shaggy body, and stroked his old head until he calmed down.

"I'm glad to see you too, mate," I whispered, hugging him tight, remembering the skinny dogs I'd seen in war-torn France; desperately trying to survive in the desolate streets.

"Come on, fellow. Let's go home," I said finally, rising and heading toward the new bridge. The wind shook the trees and the rush of water seemed unusually loud as I stepped onto the bridge. Suddenly Shep was in front of me, barking furiously and tugging at my pant leg.

"What's wrong, boy?" I asked, bewildered. "Don't you want to go home?"

I started forward again, but Shep barked even louder and blocked my steps with his shaggy body. *Not this way,* he seemed to say. *I don't like this bridge.*

The anxiety Shep betrayed was as fervent as the joy he'd shown when he first saw me. It was obvious that my dog was not going to cross the new bridge, and he didn't want me to cross it either.

I stood stock-still, staring at Shep in confusion. He barked again and darted forward to pull at my pant leg, trying to drag me off the new bridge.

"Don't you like the new bridge?" I asked him. "Does it scare you?"

Shep gazed up at me imploringly and whined. He was using the same look of longing that he'd successfully used on me as a puppy whenever he wanted a bite from my dinner plate. I couldn't resist it.

I laughed. "Okay, silly beast. We'll go the old way, for auld lang syne. But tomorrow you and I are crossing the new bridge together so that you won't be afraid anymore. Can't have my old pal afraid of a little ol' bridge!"

Shep was mighty relieved when I turned my steps back to the river road. We walked companionably down the road, across the old girder bridge, and along the lane toward home. I kept dropping my hand down to scratch my dog behind the ears as my eyes searched eagerly for the light from the kitchen window. And there it was! I could see Mama bending over the old stove. It looked like she was taking a pie out of the oven. My timing couldn't have been more perfect!

I broke into a run, and Shep accompanied me right up to the front lawn. I barely registered the fact that he turned away as I bolted up the front walk and burst into the door without knocking, shouting: "Mama! Dad! I'm home!" I was overwhelmed by the smell of cinnamon and apple and the intangible something that I always associated with home.

I heard the sound of a plate crashing to the floor in the kitchen. Then Mama stood in the doorway, her eyes like saucers. "Joe? Joey?" She ran to me, and I swept her up into my arms and whirled her around and around. Then Dad raced into the room and grabbed the two of us in a bear hug. A moment later, my little sister came running down the stairs, tears streaming across her freckled cheeks as she welcomed me home.

The next few minutes were a chaos of shouting and laughing and crying and pounding one another on the back. Finally, my practical Mama pulled everyone into the kitchen, picked up the broken plate, and then served everyone warm apple pie with ice cream.

I took a huge mouthful of apple pie. Bliss. Swallowing, I said with my mouth full of crumbs, "I would have been here sooner, but old Shep made me take the long way around. He doesn't like that new bridge they built over the river."

I took a swallow of cold milk and then noticed that everyone was staring at me strangely.

"Old Shep?" asked my Dad, carefully putting down his fork.

"Yes. He came to meet me on the river road. Good old boy! But for some reason, he didn't want me crossing the new bridge. Seemed scared of it. Did something happen to him on that bridge?"

Everyone was staring at me. Mama had gone pale, and my sister's eyes were all pupil. "What's wrong?" I asked, alarmed.

"Old Shep is dead, son," my Dad said finally. "He died last winter."

My stomach lurched, and my arms crawled with chills. *Died last winter?*

"But I saw him," I said, my voice high and tight. "Out by the bridge. I'm not lying, Pop."

"I believe you son," my father said hastily. "Maybe we'd better take a look at the new bridge in the morning to see why Shep didn't want you to walk on it."

I nodded uncertainly and then finished my dessert.

After breakfast the next morning, I followed my dad down to the river. It didn't take long to reach the new bridge, and what we saw frightened the breath out of me. The center of the bridge was completely washed away, and the swollen floodwaters thundered forcefully right below it. Twisted sharp bits along the edges of the cut showed where the force of the flood had torn the bridge to pieces.

My dad swallowed hard as his gaze traveled slowly back and forth along the broken pieces of bridge. "You never would have seen the gap in the dark," he whispered.

"No," I agreed shakily. My knees were wobbling and my stomach churned at the thought. I would have walked right off the bridge and been swept away in the flooded river. There was no way even the strongest swimmer could have survived in the debris-filled floodwaters. I'd have survived the beaches of Normandy only to die on the road home if it hadn't been for old Shep. Poor dead Shep, who'd come back from the grave to make sure I'd make it home.

"Good dog," said my dad, his voice choked with tears. "Good dog."

And just for an instant, I thought I heard old Shep give a soft bark of joy.

5

Old House Woods

I sat bolt upright in bed, heart pounding, sure I'd heard a sound. Beside me, my wife—normally a heavy sleeper—was moving restlessly on her pillow. She'd heard it too. Then it came again, a frantic knocking on the front door. I ran to my window, which looked down over the front stoop, and thrust it open.

"Who's there?" I shouted.

The fellow looked up from his frantic knocking, and I recognized the face of my neighbor Adam in the moonlight.

"Jesse, thank God!" he gasped, clutching at his side as if he'd run all the way from his house to mine. "My daughter is terribly sick. High fever, delirium. Would you go for the doctor?"

Adam was a waterman and didn't own a horse.

"Of course I'll go, just soon as I get old Tom hitched to the buggy," I called down to him.

"Thank ya, Jesse. Thank ya!" Adam called. He raced back down the lane, obviously anxious to get back to his wife and daughter.

I pulled my head in the window and hurried to dress. My wife, roused by all the shouting, followed me downstairs and made me wrap up warm against the chilly autumn air. I had old

OLD HOUSE WOODS

Tom hitched to the buggy lickety-split and soon was jogging down the rough road heading toward the doctor's house, which was on the far side of Old House Woods.

And that's when it hit me. I was going to drive through Old House Woods in the middle of the night! The thought made my teeth rattle and chills run up and down my arms. Old House Woods—not a place I'd mess about in under normal circumstances. But little Ellie, Adam's daughter, was a frequent customer of the candy section of my store, and I didn't want anything bad to happen to the blue-eyed tot.

As soon as I got to a smooth section of road, I urged old Tom to go faster. We jostled over roots and ruts as quickly as we could go safely, and the rattling of the buggy (and my bones!) almost, but not quite, drove out the stories I'd heard all my life about Old House Woods.

Folks in these parts said the woods were haunted, though they disagreed on exactly who was doing the haunting. Some said that the ghosts were buccaneers who had buried their treasure in the woods. The buccaneers had, unluckily, met Blackbeard himself on their way out of the bay and had lost both their treasure map and their life to the king of pirates. It was rumored that their ghosts drove Blackbeard away before he could claim their treasure and that the buccaneers still haunted Old House Woods to this day, determined to keep their treasure a secret.

An older variation of the story claimed that the ghosts of Old House Woods were soldiers sent to the Colony of Virginia by Charles II of England after his defeat at the Battle of Worcester in 1651. The soldiers were tasked with guarding a ship full of treasure, and all went well until the ship docked in

Chesapeake Bay. About half the treasure had been unloaded and carried to a secret stash in the woods when renegades attacked the crew of the treasure ship, killing sailors and soldiers alike and making away with as much of the treasure as remained in the ship. Unfortunately for the renegades, a sudden storm in the Chesapeake capsized the ship, killing everyone on board. Folks wandering the Old House Woods at night claim that the Royalist soldiers can still be seen stalking the lanes and byways, guarding the treasure chests that still remain under their care, while a ghostly treasure ship comes sailing in from the bay and rises up out of the water to glide over the tops of the trees.

A third iteration of the tale claimed that British soldiers, after smuggling a large chest full of money and gold through American lines during the Revolutionary War, found that the ship they were to meet had capsized in a Chesapeake storm. The soldiers buried the treasure in Old House Woods, planning to claim it after the war was won. Instead they died in the battle of Yorktown, and it was their ghosts who returned to the wood to haunt the place where their treasure was buried.

I shuddered a bit at the thought and slowed Old Tom. We'd reached a particularly rutted stretch of road, and Old House Woods with its pirate/Royalist/British ghosts lay directly ahead. The trees loomed dark against the starry sky, and the long branches, bare of leaves, looked like skeletal hands stretching toward my face. I didn't like the look of the place at all. But it was the fastest way to town, and little Ellie was ill. So I boldly drove straight into Old House Woods.

Above me, the wind moaned in the treetops, whipping the branches to and fro. I urged old Tom forward, and woods closed in around us, dark and full of strange crackling noises and sudden sharp reports. *Acorns falling to the ground,* I thought sagely. *And night creatures going about their natural business.*

A cool night breeze crept into the buggy with a whooshing sound that sounded almost like a moan. The hairs on my neck twitched, and I shuddered a little. *Silly fancies,* I told myself.

And then I saw a light ahead of me. I at first thought someone was walking through the woods with a lantern, but the light didn't look like a lantern. For one thing, it bobbed up and down in a manner quite unlike a person walking. And it was blue. I'd never seen a blue lantern in these parts.

The cold wind was back, slithering around me with icy fingers. My teeth began to chatter and my hands shook on the reins. I pressed against the seat, glad to have something guarding my back. I should call out a greeting to the walker. It was the polite thing to do. But I couldn't force my voice past the lump in my throat.

The woods around me had gone still. No animals rustled; no acorns dropped. Even the wind was gone. Old Tom snorted suddenly and stopped walking. He shied a little in the traces, his head held high, nostrils flaring in fear.

"C . . . come on Tom," I croaked through the lump in my throat, though the last thing I wanted to do was move closer to that ghostly light. I shook the reins several times, and finally, his body quivering with reluctance, Old Tom moved forward along the road.

And then I saw the source of the blue light. Old Tom stopped and braced all four feet. He wasn't going any farther, and I didn't blame him. In front of us, walking a few inches off the ground, was a Royalist soldier in full armor. He shone from within, helmet and breastplate sparkling with small dancing stars of blue light. He held an old-fashioned gun over one shoulder and marched briskly as if he were on guard duty.

Fear tore the breath from my throat. I thought my heart would beat right out of my chest, and—in spite of the cold—my whole body dripped with sweat. I wanted to leap from the buggy and run screaming from the woods, but my legs and arms were frozen in place.

Suddenly the soldier turned and looked straight at me. More ghostly figures appeared, their bodies glittering with sparkling lights. They wore armor, like the guard in front of me, and they carried guns and a few shovels. They were heading toward a dead pine tree about a hundred yards from the buggy. As soon as they reached it, the ones carrying shovels began to dig.

The soldier in front of me slowly drew the sword that had—until that moment—lain unnoticed at his side. He grinned wickedly at me, and I suddenly realized that he had no skin. His face was a skeleton with glowing blue-white eyes. The armor under the starry lights was completely clear, showing bones and sinews underneath.

Gulping in horror, I pressed back against the seat in the bitter-cold air. The soldier walked toward me, sword raised. I screamed, scrambling sideways. Old Tom screamed too—a terrible horsey scream. Caught off balance, I pitched into the back of the buggy and found myself looking up into the glowing eye-sockets of the skeletal soldier. Then everything went black.

A long while later, I heard my wife calling my name. I stirred and opened my eyes to bright sunshine and the cheerful chirp of birds. I was at home in my bed, and all was well.

At least all was well until the memory of the events of the preceding night came back to me. I sat bolt upright with a yelp of fear. "The ghost! I saw a ghost," I babbled. I jumped up and began pacing the room, wringing my hands together and muttering to myself.

It took my wife nearly ten minutes to calm me down. She explained that they'd gone looking for me when I didn't return. They found Old Tom trembling at the turn of the road just beyond Old House Woods, hitched to an apparently empty buggy. When they check the buggy, they found me lying unconscious on the floor. They'd led Old Tom home and put him in the barn, still hitched to the buggy because he was too terrified to let anyone near him, while one of my sons saddled up another horse and went to fetch the doctor for little Ellie.

I told my wife the whole story, and to my astonishment she believed me. *Everyone* knew Old House Woods was haunted, she said. And now we knew which tale was true.

Every time I thought about the old Royalist ghosts guarding their treasure, my hair stood on end and chills ran all over my body. I was never going through the woods again at night. Never!

That reminded me of Old Tom, who was still hitched to the buggy; the boys couldn't get near him. I went out to the barn with several apples and a pocket full of sugar cubes—and it took every last one of them to get Tom calmed down and unhitched. I was never able to get him close to Old House Woods again. He'd brace all four legs and refuse to budge as soon as we came in sight of the woods, trembling from head to tail. It was months before I could lead him anywhere near the woods, and then it took an enormous number of sugar cubes just to make him take the road around it. Can't say that I blame him—not after what we'd seen.

The good news was that the doctor reached little Ellie in time. She had a close shave, but a month later she was back at my store, carefully counting out her pennies to buy sweets. So things ended happily after all.

6

A Love Betrayed

Ann was a beauty, and she knew it. Not a good combination. Add to that a fiery temper, and it was a wonder that she married at all. But somehow she managed to persuade one suitor to accompany her to the altar. Which frankly amazed her friends and family.

The man was one Peyton Skipworth, a wealthy planter. He took his new bride home to his plantation, where they settled down to an aristocratic life of ease, comfort, and arguing. Marriage had done nothing to soften Ann's temper.

She and Peyton blossomed out into society during the early days of their marriage and frequently visited the capital city of Williamsburg. But as time went on, they did not always stay in the same house. Peyton began taking rooms at a local tavern, while Ann stayed as a guest at a neighboring house. All was not well in paradise.

One year, Ann and Peyton were invited to a gala ball at the Governor's Palace. It was a grand event, and all of society would be there—including Ann's pretty sister, Jean. That created quite a problem for Ann. On Jean's last visit to the plantation, Ann had noticed Peyton noticing Jean. Ann had caused quite a scene.

A LOVE BETRAYED

Jean had been very embarrassed by her vituperative sister and had cut her visit short. Peyton had been enigmatic, admitting nothing and denying nothing, which had done nothing to quell Ann's outrage.

Unfortunately for Ann, the governor's ball was the event of the season. Everyone was going, and it would cause talk if the Skipworths missed it. Peyton insisted that they attend, and Ann was forced to go along. Determined to show a happy face to the world, Ann spent a great deal of time over her dress that day. She was staying at the Wythe house on this particular visit, and her husband met her there to escort her to the ball. Ann was resplendent in cream satin, and on her feet she wore red slippers with buckles of brilliants. Knowing she looked her best, Ann took her husband's proffered arm, and they made their way together to the Governor's Palace in the company of many of the wealthy and important members of society.

At first, all went well. Ann danced and mingled and laughed. Then one of her so-called friends started talking about how fond Peyton seemed to be of her sister, Jean. The woman's words were innocent enough, but her tone and look spoke volumes. Ann feigned indifference, but as soon as the woman was gone, she flushed with anger. She had expressly warned her husband to stay away from Jean, but he had not heeded her warning. Now the cream of Virginia society was gossiping about it. This was not to be borne!

Ann crossed the room in high dudgeon and confronted her husband right on the dance floor. Peyton pulled her to one side and stood his ground, smiling his enigmatic smile while she berated him. He didn't even tell her to keep her voice down, which was infuriating. Worse, he did not deny her accusations, which grew wilder by the moment. People in their section of the ballroom were turning to stare at them, but Peyton still stood calmly gazing at his acrimonious wife.

"Ann, calm yourself. You're making a scene," a familiar voice hissed from a nearby doorway. Ann turned and saw her sister standing only a few yards away. That was the last straw. She turned bright red, pointed at her sister, and gasped, "You . . . you . . . " The words choked in her throat. Ann turned bright red and trembled with rage and hurt, feeling utterly betrayed by both her sister and her husband.

Suddenly overcome by her feelings, Ann fled from the ballroom as the orchestra struck up another minuet. She raced passed groups of laughing guests and burst through the front doors of the palace. Holding up her skirts in one hand, she ran right out onto the grass, tears of rage pouring down her cheeks. As she ran, her heel caught in a hole in the lawn and the strap of her slipper broke. Unheeding, she ran on, leaving her red slipper behind in the grass. By the time she reached the Wythe house, her silk stocking was torn and dirty.

Bursting inside, Ann raced upstairs on uneven feet, her slipper clicking noisily and her stocking foot silent: Click-thump. Click-thump. She sounded like a person trying to run with a peg leg, but she hardly noticed the strange sound as it echoed through the house. She wanted Peyton to come after her, to tell her that her suspicions were unfounded. But she knew he wouldn't come. She'd lost her husband's heart to her sister.

Ann cried herself to sleep that night, and she moped about the next day, feeling both ill and ill-used. But there was nothing anyone could say or do to comfort her. She knew the truth, and it broke her proud heart.

Still, Peyton remained her husband, and when their stay in Williamsburg came to an end, Ann returned with him to their plantation home. Outwardly, life resumed a normal pattern. Nothing more was said between them about Jean or their argument at the ball. Not that Peyton would have spoken anyway, Ann thought bitterly, feeling the familiar sick sensation in her stomach.

Shortly after they arrived home, Ann realized that her frequent bouts of illness were not caused by thoughts of her sister and husband. The pattern was too regular and the nausea came mostly in the morning. Soon it was confirmed that Ann was in the family way.

Peyton seemed pleased by the news. The expectation of a child brought the couple closer, and Ann was almost happy in the short months that followed. But the baby came much too early, and the pain was agonizing. The child was stillborn, and Ann could find no peace in mind, body, or soul. All she could think about was Jean. Jean and Peyton. Jean . . . and Peyton . . . until she thought no more.

The midwife brought the news of Ann's death to her husband. He took it stoically, as he had taken everything that Ann had ever dished out to him. No one seeing him at that moment would have guessed that his thoughts went immediately to Ann's sister.

Peyton married Jean after a very brief period of mourning, and the couple settled down in the plantation home that Ann had made so uncomfortable during her short duration as mistress. It was obvious to all who saw them that they were well matched and happy together. All was well in paradise—until the day a rumor reached the ears of the new Lady Skipworth. People in Williamsburg were saying that the ghost of Ann Skipworth had been seen in the Wythe house, wearing the cream-colored gown she'd worn to the governor's ball and primping in an upstairs mirror. Later, around midnight, her spirit could be heard running up the staircase to her bedroom, one slippered foot clicking its heel on the wooden staircase while the other stocking-clad foot thudded beside it. Scandalmongers said that Ann's restless spirit was reliving the fateful moment when she realized that she had lost her husband to her sister. And maybe it was true.

The rumor became so widespread that it made life quite uncomfortable for the newlyweds whenever they visited Williamsburg. So the new Lady Skipworth was very pleased when Virginia's capital was moved to Richmond in 1780. It meant that she no longer had to attend society events in Williamsburg.

Lady Ann's spirit never left Williamsburg. She can still be heard at midnight, climbing the staircase of the Wythe house wearing only one shoe, forever reliving the moment when she realized her love had been betrayed.

7

I Will Find Her

Jared couldn't believe it when his fiancée Bethany fell ill just a few short weeks before their marriage. She was a strong, healthy girl—the daughter of his neighbor—but she just faded away before his eyes. He tried everything he could to save her, contacting the local physician and even riding his horse many weary miles to get a specialist from the city. But nothing could be done. The pain radiated out from her middle so intensely that the local doctor decided to keep her on morphine at all times.

There came a day when Jared refused to leave Bethany's side, knowing that at any moment she could go. He slept in a chair during the night and sat on the side of her bed during the day. She was so heavily drugged that she didn't recognize him until her final moments. The morning before they were to have wed, she called his name, and her eyes cleared for the first time since she fell ill. Jared took her into his arms, and they spoke quietly of the life they would have together "someday." He held her long after she gasped out her last breath.

Jared was inconsolable. Long after Bethany's body lay buried beside the Great Dismal Swamp, he sat alone in his room,

I WILL FIND HER

grieving for his lost love. He scorned food and sleep, depriving himself until his mind gave way under the strain. One morning, he came out into the kitchen as happy as he had been before Bethany's tragic illness. His mother was delighted at first, until something in his conversation revealed that he had lost touch with reality and thought that his betrothed was still alive. Jared now believed that Bethany had gone away for awhile because of a tiff with her parents, but he was sure that he could mend the rift between them.

"I will find her and apologize for them. Then she'll come home with me and we'll be married," he told his mother earnestly. "I will find her, Mama."

His family tried to reason with him, but Jared's mind was made up. His Bethany was missing, not dead, and he would listen to no one who suggested otherwise. He spent the majority of every day walking up and down the highways and byways, calling her name. After about a week, he became obsessed with the notion that she was living somewhere in the swamp, perhaps in one of the abandoned fishing shacks. She would never wish to be far from her parents, in spite of the breach he imagined between them.

"I will find her," he told his anxious family, passionate in his conviction. "I will find her and bring her home."

Something in his mother's expression worried him. He stepped forward and took her hand. "She is ill, Mama, and tired. I think she is afraid she is going to die."

His mother brightened a little with hope. This was the first time Jared had acknowledged that something more than an argument might have sent his Bethany from him.

"Don't worry," Jared continued. "I will hide her away from Death so that he will never find her when he comes."

His eyes blazed with an insane fire that repelled his family. His mother tore her hands from his and turned away from the madness she could no longer deny. She covered her face with her hands, her body tense with pain.

Jared's father tried once again to convince him that his beloved lay dead beside the swamp, but Jared would not listen. He broke away from his father violently and ran off to the Great Dismal Swamp. Jared wandered about for days, living on roots and berries and sleeping at night in the dank marshland. Endlessly, he called out to his beloved to come to him, but there was no answer.

One evening at dusk, Jared went out to Lake Drummond, an expanse of water in the middle of the Dismal Swamp. On the black surface of the water, he saw the soft blinking of fireflies dancing hither and thither across the black surface.

To his dazed eyes, the soft lights framed a beloved figure that beckoned to him wistfully and called out his name.

"Bethany, my love!" he exclaimed, overjoyed. "I see her life-light!"

To his maddened mind, it seemed that Bethany hovered over the waters, her spirit caught between this world and the next. A gesture either way would determine whether she lived or died. He saw her life-candle flickering behind her, growing more erratic and burning down toward nothing. If he didn't reach her in time, the candle would burn out, and she would be lost to him forever.

Jared, who could not swim, rushed around, frantically constructing a raft of cypress branches so that he could reach his love before she disappeared. Lashing the branches together with vines, he leapt on top of the flimsy craft and floated out to join the girl he had lost. As he drew near the center of the pond, a wind sprang up, and the raft was tossed and tumbled in the sudden waves. With a cry of alarm, Jared fell from the raft and sank down into the murky waters. He thrashed about desperately, his eyes on the fireflies dancing above the water, just out of reach.

"Bethany!" he screamed, the name choking off as water filled his mouth. "Beth . . . " The last bit was lost as his head went under for the final time.

The next day, Jared's drowned body was found by his father, who had come searching for his insane child. The family buried him next to Bethany.

Occasionally, visitors to Lake Drummond still hear Jared's voice echoing dismally across the still waters as he searches for his beloved. And some brave souls who remain in the vicinity after dark claim that the phantoms of Jared and Bethany, reunited in death, sometimes float across the pond on a raft made of cypress branches, carrying a firefly lantern to light their way.

Elbow Road

VIRGINIA BEACH

I hadn't heard about the unsolved mystery in my town until after I started dating Tanya. On our very first date, she got real excited when she learned I came from Virginia Beach and asked me if the mystery of Mrs. Woble had ever been solved. I stared at her blankly. I'd never even heard of Mrs. Woble, never mind any unsolved mystery surrounding her. How *Tanya* knew such a story was a mystery to me.

When I asked her about it, her face lit up in delight. Apparently she was a big fan of unsolved mysteries and collected every newspaper article and book on the topic she could lay hands on. That's how she'd learned the tragic tale of Mrs. Woble.

"She lived in an isolated house on Elbow Road in Chesapeake, or maybe it was on the Virginia Beach side. I don't remember the details," Tanya said briskly. "Surely you've heard about her?"

Surely I hadn't. Oh, I'd heard of Elbow Road, all right. I'd even driven there on a dare. Elbow Road is supposed to be haunted, and growing up in Virginia Beach I'd heard all about the phantom jogger who runs along a certain stretch of the road

ELBOW ROAD

and then vanishes into thin air. They say a truck slammed into him and the driver didn't stop to help. An eyewitness called the police, but the jogger died before he made it to the hospital; his dog was never found. Folks say his ghost still jogs along Elbow Road searching for his dog.

And then there are the phantom footsteps. If you park your car on the curve near Stumpy Lake around midnight, child-size glowing footsteps will walk toward you. They appear in the dust alongside the road and sometimes appear on the pavement. The footprints on the road look wet and soggy, as if the phantom were walking in the rain. One story behind the footprints says that a car went off the road in a huge storm, killing two girls inside it—an infant and a young teenager. Another states that a little girl drowned in the nearby lake while fishing with her father. Whichever story is true, I've had several friends check it out. All of them have seen the glowing footprints.

But the story of the disappearing Mrs. Woble was new to me. I asked Tanya for details.

Mrs. Woble lived alone on a rather isolated curve on Elbow Road. One week she disappeared from her home. Her neighbors and friends became concerned when they didn't hear from her for a few days, and they called the police.

The authorities found that the back door of the house had been forced open and glass lay all over the floor. The lights were still burning in the hall, and the overhead light and the TV were on in the living room.

The police called out for Mrs. Woble, but no one responded. They began searching the house. They found an untouched dinner plate on the dining room table; the food was congealed and beginning to go bad. Her car keys sat on a small table by the front door, so she obviously hadn't driven anywhere. It was puzzling.

"Maybe she's hurt," one officer murmured to the other. "Maybe she fell down and hit her head?"

"What about the forced door?" the other asked grimly.

"She could have lost her keys," the first officer said, without conviction.

"Let's check upstairs," said his companion.

Armed, the men cautiously went upstairs. The first room they checked was empty. But when they opened the door of the second—Mrs. Woble's bedroom—they were overwhelmed by the stench of blood. Dried blood spattered the walls and floor. Furniture was overturned and knocked awry. It looked as if a terrible murder had taken place in that room. But there was no body, only blood and gore.

The case of the vanished Mrs. Woble was never solved. The house was put up for sale, but such was its grim reputation that it never sold and had to be torn down.

At the conclusion of the tale, Tanya burbled, "I'd love to see the place. Maybe look around for clues."

"How can you find clues in a torn-down house?" I asked skeptically. "Besides, this must have been years ago. If the police didn't find any clues, what makes you think you can?"

"Still, I'd like to see it," Tanya said stubbornly. She looked so cute with her lip thrust out and her eyes sparkling with defiance that I volunteered to take her to Elbow Road the next time I went home on break. She eagerly accepted.

After all, I consoled myself when I considered the wild goose chase we were planning, it gave me a chance to introduce my parents to their future daughter-in-law. Not that I'd told Tanya my future wedding plans. I didn't want to scare her off.

Tanya and I went home to Virginia Beach around Christmas time to spend the holidays with my folks. They loved Tanya right away. My father cornered me in the kitchen and ordered me not to foul things up with this one because—and I quote—"she's a keeper, son." I solemnly promised not to foul things up. It was a promise I intended to keep, which meant that I was going to have to drive Tanya down to Elbow Road and explore some ruined old house, looking for clues to an unsolved mystery.

Tanya was so excited at the idea that I volunteered to drive her along Elbow Road that night, even though it was already dark, just to give her a feel for the scene. We'd do our serious exploring in the morning. Tanya immediately raced out the front door and jumped into my car. She was so excited, she forgot to put on her coat! I laughed, grabbed her jacket and mine, and followed her out to the car.

A few minutes later, we made the turn onto Elbow Road. The headlights glowed in the darkness, and I kept the speed slow, remembering the curves that had claimed more than one life on this winding, wooded road.

"Wow, this place is really creepy," Tanya said.

Some of the enthusiasm had left from her voice as the trees lining the narrow road leaned down over the car, their bare branches stretching toward us like demon fingers. A gust of wind shook the windows, and the air inside the car seemed cold and clammy in spite of the warmth blasting from the heater. For some reason, all I could think of was Mrs. Woble's bedroom blood-spattered walls. It made me shudder in the darkness of the car.

"I don't know which curve she lived on," Tanya said, her voice sounding weak and thin in the coldness of the car. "We may not be able to see the ruins in the dark. Maybe we should come back in the daylight."

I could scarcely believe my ears. What had happened to my bold, crazy girlfriend? Of course this was a creepy stretch of road, even in daylight. After dark, it was positively menacing. Any minute, I expected someone to leap out of the shadows with an ax and fling himself at the car.

Even as this image crossed my mind, I rounded the next curve. My headlights caught the figure of a plump woman in a pale-colored dress limping desperately along the side of the road. She was covered in blood, and her head hung grotesquely to one side as though her neck had been broken. Tanya screamed, and I hit the brakes. The headlights passed right through the woman's translucent body. She was a ghost!

"Dear God! Dear God!" Tanya screamed, wringing her hands. "It's Mrs. Woble!"

The phantom did not seem to notice our car. She kept stumbling toward a flickering light on the far side of the curve. Goose bumps prickled all over my skin, and I shuddered violently as I watched the desperate figure approach the flickering light. Before my eyes, the light grew taller and wider. It became the flat, two-dimensional outline of a house among the trees.

Tanya moaned in sheer terror as the bloodstained figure lurched toward the black-and-white outline of the house. The tormented phantom was half walking, half-crawling in her desperation to get home. When her bloody fingertips touched the porch railing, house and phantom vanished, leaving a chilling darkness behind.

The horror freezing us in place released us.

"Get us out of here now!" Tanya commanded, her voice high and tight.

Having no desire to linger in that haunted spot, I did a U-turn, spinning out my wheels. Desperate to leave Elbow Road, I raced back home at a dangerous speed for such a winding road. It was only when we reached a well-lit main road that I slowed the car a little and took a shuddering breath of relief.

Neither of us spoke on the drive home. It was only when we were safely in my driveway that Tanya said: "So she was murdered after all. It must have been her blood the police found on the walls."

I didn't say anything. What was there to say? I loosened my hands on the steering wheel. I'd gripped it so tightly that I'd bruised all along the inside of my knuckles.

I drew in several deep breaths and finally asked, "Do you still want to go investigating tomorrow?" My voice came out so high and thin that I didn't recognize it.

"No!" Tanya almost shouted the word. "My verdict: death by homicide. Case closed!" She scrambled out of the car almost as fast as she'd entered it and bolted into the safety of the house.

I exited the car with exaggerated slowness. My hands were still trembling, and I wasn't sure my jelly legs would carry me to the house. I leaned against the car door, pondering what we had just witnessed. That we'd seen the ghost of Mrs. Woble I had no doubt. At least, it fit the story as Tanya had related it to me. And I was convinced that if we returned to that particular curve on Elbow Road, we'd find the ruined foundations of a house there—one that looked just like the strange two-dimensional

cutout house toward which the phantom had crawled. But seeing the ghost didn't solve the mystery. From the evidence found in her bedroom, we'd already assumed that Mrs. Woble had been murdered. Seeing her phantom just confirmed the hypothesis. It didn't explain what had happened to her, who had done it, or why.

I finally followed Tanya inside. In the end, it wasn't my problem to solve. If the police couldn't find the killer, no one could. It would remain an unsolved mystery—just the way my girlfriend liked them.

The thought of Tanya's obsession made me smile. And my grin broadened as I realized that I wouldn't be spending my holidays digging fruitlessly among the ruins of a house on Elbow Road. Thank you, Mrs. Woble.

9

Shower of Stones

NEWPORT

I don't reckon folks will believe the story I've got to tell. But I swear on a stack of Bibles that it's the truth, so help me God. I was a slave back in them days, working for Doc McChesney on his plantation-farm called Greenwood. I was working as a kitchen assistant and general housemaid when the troubles began. And they were amazing troubles, let me tell you.

It all started with a young slave gal named Maria. We heard her screaming something awful out in the yard. A minute later she came running into the parlor where Missus McChesney was rocking the baby. Maria was cryin' her eyes out, and her teeth were chattering with fear. She looked terrible, with welts and bruises all over. When we asked her how she got all beat up, she claimed an old woman had appeared in the yard and started beating on her. The old woman had chased her right up to the house; she just barely got away. Poor Maria could barely speak, she was so afraid.

A bunch of us went running out into the yard armed with rolling pins and brooms and such, ready to do battle with the old woman. But no one was there. We searched all the outbuildings and found nothing.

SHOWER OF STONES

But that weren't nothing compared to what happened next. I was walking through the yard one, maybe two days later when a huge chunk of mud came hurling toward me out of nowhere. Hit me square in the chest and just about ruined my best shirt. Furious, I started shouting and looking around for the culprit. But I was alone in the yard. My yells brought the mistress of the house to the door, and we both saw—swear to God—two more huge clumps of mud rise up off the ground and propel themselves across the yard. I had to duck to avoid getting more mud on my shirt. The mistress was staring with her mouth open in shock. She beckoned to me to run into the house quick. I didn't need telling twice. I was across the yard lickety-split, and I heard two more mud clots hit the kitchen door just after I slammed it shut.

Inside the house, Cook told me that someone—or rather something—had been throwing sizzling hot rocks. The rocks had already knocked over a pitcher full of water, broken a vase of flowers, and put some mighty big dents in the furniture.

We were all afraid of the ghost or phantom or whatever it was throwing mud and rocks around. Over the next few days, it really got active. We all had to duck more than once when objects came flying out of nowhere, but the spirit seemed particularly attentive to little Maria. She'd be working quietly at the kitchen table or dusting in the parlor when all at once she'd start shrieking and crying and fall right on the floor. She said something was beating on her. We could all hear the spirit slapping her, and we all saw bruises and welts forming on her face and arms out of nowhere.

First time it happened, I ran forward and tried to stop the creature, but it gave me such a slap that I flew backward and rolled head over heels, landing with a bang at the feet of the mistress, who'd just come in the door. After that, she told us to stay away from Maria if we saw the spirit pummeling her. She didn't want anyone else getting hurt by the phantom.

The doctor thought the whole thing was nonsense. He said Maria was just pretending in order to get attention, and he blamed the rock and mud throwing on hoodlums.

But things got even worse. Whole showers of stones started raining down on the roof. Sounded just like rapid gunfire the first time it happened. We thought we were under attack by marauders, and a bunch of us crowded underneath the kitchen table, quaking with fear. After the shower of stones had stopped, we ventured outside to see the damage. The yard was littered with rocks the size of a man's fist. That first shower of stones happened after dark, but it wasn't long before they were coming in daylight too.

It puzzled me how the doctor could blame the attacks on hoodlums. Anyone brave enough to venture outside when the rocks started flyin' could see that there wasn't anyone there to throw them. It wasn't always showers. Sometimes just one or two rocks came hurling out of the sky. Some of those rocks were big! They weighed too much to be tossed about by an ordinary fellow, not even the blacksmith.

All these supernatural happenings soon caught the attention of folks in the nearby towns. Folks started trespassing on our property, hoping to see the Devil's handiwork for themselves. It made Doctor McChesney furious to have all those strangers lurking about. At first it was just a few folks from the nearby regions. But word spread, and hundreds of folks began traveling from all over to see the stone showers at the farm. The doctor quickly abandoned his usual courtesy toward strangers and drove curiosity-seekers away with such yelling and cursing that they fled the property as fast as they could. Some of them swore they'd seen the Devil himself on the farm and told everyone they'd barely escaped with their lives. But what they'd really seen was the doctor in a rage.

'Course, when a wagonload of church elders arrived, the doctor and his missus welcomed them politely and invited them to stay for dinner. Oh my, we enjoyed seeing the look on their faces when a sharp black stone came flying down from the ceiling and cut one of their biscuits clean in half. They were amazed, frightened too. Never saw folks exit a house so quick after a meal, and with the barest courtesies. I'd have been indignant on behalf of my master and mistress if I hadn't found it so funny.

That evening Mrs. McChesney started beggin' her husband to move away from the devil-ridden house. Of course the doctor refused. In spite of the almost daily stone showers and the mud flinging and Maria's beatings, he still maintained that nothing was wrong at Greenwood. But the mistress was convinced that the Devil was behind the incidents at the farm and that he would keep plaguing them until they left the premises or until Maria—who seemed to be the main target of the attacks—was sent away.

A few days after the elders' visit, Maria was outside on the porch pouting on account of Cook wouldn't give her a snack when a bunch of floppy round circles appeared out of nowhere and pummeled her from all sides. I saw the whole thing through the open kitchen door and let out a yell. Cook and me and some of the McChesney children ran out onto the porch and stared at Maria, who was covered with pancakes! That'll teach her to snack before dinner!

Then the spirit started plaguing the McChesney baby. And I didn't find that funny at all. Little James was lying in his cradle when he suddenly began crying and tossing about like a mad thing. I was making beds upstairs when I heard him scream out. When both his mama and I ran into the room to check on him, we saw him rolling about wildly as tiny red pinpricks of blood appeared all over his little body. We screamed for the doctor.

"I want that girl sent away right now!" Missus McChesney said to her husband once the baby settled down a bit. She was in such a frenzy that the doctor reluctantly agreed to send Maria to stay at the home of his brother-in-law.

Maria left the next mornin' with a small satchel of clothes and some food to eat on the long walk. All that day, the house was plumb quiet. No stones hit the roof; no mud flew through the yard. And the red pinpricks disappeared like magic from baby James. Everything was so peaceful and still, we couldn't believe it. Then Maria came walking back into the yard late in the evening. Almost at once, a big ol' rock crashed into the roof of the house.

Everyone was so surprised to see her! We crowded out onto the porch, demanding to know why she'd come on back. She told us that the spirit had followed her to the other house. As soon as Maria came in sight of the brother-in-law's place, she heard a sound like the galloping of a dozen horses. The family all rushed into the house and found every darned stick of furniture piled up in the center of the floor! Rocks and clods of mud appeared out of thin air and hurled themselves at them too. Just then the doctor's brother-in-law saw Maria through the parlor window. He yelled at her to go back home at once, which she did. She had nowhere else to go.

I saw the look on the mistress's face when she heard Maria's story. She was terrible afraid. But what could she do? Her husband wouldn't move away or sell Maria. He didn't believe anything was wrong at Greenwood.

Things got real bad after Maria's return. That terrible spirit beat her almost daily, and the showers of rocks battered the roof nearly to pieces. Stones and clots of mud hurled themselves randomly inside the house. They came from every which way—ceiling, floor, walls! And the yard was no safer than the house.

Doctor McChesney saw all them things happening and still refused to believe that an evil spirit had invaded the house.

And then the baby got worse. Little James suffered repeatedly from seizures, and the pinpricks reappeared on his body. His convulsions grew so bad that his mother could barely hold him. Once while Mrs. McChesney rocked little James, a chair walked itself across the room and stopped beside her as if it wanted to look at the baby in her arms. She ran to the far side of the room, and that darned chair followed her. With a scream of terror, she ran clean out of the house and wouldn't come back inside until her husband came home.

The doctor still refused to leave Greenwood or to send Maria away. He insisted nothing was really wrong at the farm. He wouldn't even ask the local church for help, which was downright foolish to my way of thinkin'. If anyone could exorcise that evil spirit, it was the pastor of the church.

But the doctor wouldn't hear of it. He insisted that his little boy was suffering from a curable disease, not from some evil haunt. Day and night, while rocks and mud clots pummeled the house and yard, the doctor dosed the poor little fellow with medicine and tried everything he knew to cure him from the seizures. But they just got worse and worse until his little body was constantly aflame with bloody red pinpricks.

Then, in the middle of a terrible convulsion, little James died. And there weren't nothin' his daddy could do to save him.

Missus McChesney wept and wept when her son died. After that, she sat in silence, rocking in her chair as stones showered down on the roof of the house and rocks hurled themselves about inside. Her silence was even more terrible than her tears.

Finally, she told the doctor that she was leaving. He could go or stay as he pleased, but she and the children were done with this evil place. I peered cautiously through the open parlor door to see what the doctor would do. His face was full of deep, sad lines that hadn't been there before little James's death, and his broad shoulders were slumped in defeat. In that moment, he finally admitted—to himself as well as his wife—that something evil had taken over Greenwood.

"Please don't leave," the doctor begged his wife. "I will sell the girl and her parents, if only you will stay here with me."

Missus McChesney closed her eyes for a minute, as if she was in pain. And then she agreed.

Within a few days, Maria and her parents were sold and left Greenwood forever. From the moment Maria left the plantation, the showers of stone ceased.

Elopement

RICHMOND

My grandfather sat silently at the far end of the table, listening as my parents raged back and forth across the good china, each blaming the other for my elder sister's elopement. I sat still as a stone as the cutting remarks grew louder, rattling the glasses. How could she have run off with a sailor? Where had they met? How long had this clandestine courtship been going on?

I glanced down the table at my tall, elegant grandfather with his lion's mane of white hair and broad, imposing shoulders. Our eyes met for an instant, and I immediately realized that Grandfather knew all about my sister's elopement and that he would never share his knowledge with my parents. I dropped my gaze to my napkin to hide a grin. I'd known about my sister's romance from the start and had kept it hidden. Why should it matter whom Elaine married, as long as he was an honorable man who earned a good living and treated her well?

A mere decade ago, we Americans wrote a Declaration of Independence that said all men were created equal. If all men were created equal, than I figured it didn't matter if Elaine was a society lady and Charlie was a poor sailor. They should be allowed to marry. But my parents thought otherwise. Father

ELOPEMENT

was the younger son of a British aristocrat, and Mama had come from a wealthy Virginia family. Marrying outside one's class was just "not done" in their worldview. So Elaine had eloped with her sailor.

When dinner was finished, my grandfather rose from the table and called, "Take a walk with me, Thomas?" My father waved me away from the table with barely a glance, so I followed my grandfather into the hallway, and the servant brought our coats.

As soon as I saw the full moon outside, my heart hammered with fear. I knew exactly where we were going, for it was the same spot my grandfather visited every month on the night of the full moon. We were walking to the river overlook to sit under the tall pine at the edge of the ravine and wait for the ghost.

The trees whispered in the night wind, and the shadows lengthened around us as we approached the narrow ravine. I hated this place. I had first heard the ghost scream at the tender age of six. The haunting began with a sudden, intense silence and a sharp drop in temperature until the surrounding air felt as cold as ice. Next, a loud cracking noise sounded from the top of an old pine tree that hung precariously over the ravine, as if a huge branch had broken in two. The cracking sound was followed by a terrible scream and the heart-stopping noise of a body plummeting into the ravine. The ghostly wail ended abruptly in a terrible thump as the screaming man hit the sharp rocks at the river's edge. It was followed by a loud splash as his dead body rolled into the river. Then there was silence.

It was a horrific death scene that played out every month under the light of the full moon. I never understood why my grandfather came here each month to listen to the tragic death replay itself again and again. He'd even installed a bench under the precarious pine.

As we approached the aforementioned tree, a shock of sheer terror iced through my body. My heart leapt into my mouth when I saw a white figure stir in the shadows under the pine. My hands shook as a second shadow joined the first. Then my sister's voice called my name, and my relief was so intense that sweat poured down my neck and back as I raced to embrace her. Charlie stood next to us, beaming with delight as he shook my grandfather's hand.

"Congratulations on your marriage," the old gentleman said, waving them to a seat on the bench. Elaine and Charlie sat holding hands as moonlight streamed over the hills to the cast. I sat on the pine needles beside the bench, leaning my head against Elaine's knee and watching moonlight flickering on the babbling water several hundred feet below our perch.

"Thank you for helping us," Charlie said to my grandfather. "I would not have had the courage to propose to Elaine if you hadn't given me your approval."

"I don't understand why you approve and Mama does not," Elaine added in her soft soprano. "I thought you, of all people, would want me to marry a rich man, to bring more money or consequence to our family."

Grandfather smiled and took a seat beside Charlie. "I have more money than I know what to do with. As for consequence, that is something your mother cares about. I value other things. Like family. And love." He paused and then reached into his deep coat pocket and removed a long box, which he turned over and over in his hands. Finally, he said, "Perhaps this wedding present and the story that goes with it will help you understand why I have given my consent to your runaway marriage."

Grandfather handed the box to Elaine. I watched curiously as she opened it and drew out a long, blue-and-white-checked bandana made of gingham. The homely old scarf was covered with the most intricate embroidery I'd ever seen. Delicate flowers and graceful birds filled every inch. The flowers seemed to shimmer in the moonlight as Elaine turned it this way and that, staring in fascination at the artwork stitched upon such an unlikely object. She handed the bandana to Charlie and removed a second item from the box, a slim silver dagger with a lovely design engraved upon the hilt. Charlie passed me the embroidered bandana and took the dagger from Elaine as my grandfather began his story.

"My younger brother was a sailor like you, Charlie," Grandfather began. "His name was also Charles, and he was a lieutenant in the navy."

I stared incredulously at Grandfather's stern face in the moonlight. "I didn't know you had a brother," I exclaimed.

Grandfather frowned at me for interrupting. "He died young," Grandfather said. "If I may get back to my story?" He cocked an eyebrow at me, and I subsided onto the pine needles as he told the following tale.

Lieutenant Charles Madison was a dashing figure—tall and blond and handsome, with a roving eye and a honeyed tongue. The young ladies sighed with longing whenever Charles entered a room. He served as an aide to the admiral, and he sailed on the first Virginian flagship to enter the fabled realm of China.

One evening, the admiral and his officers were invited to dine with a powerful mandarin and his high officials. They dined in a glittering palace filled with treasures and ate the most delicious and exotic food that young Charles had ever tasted. As the meal progressed, the handsome lieutenant became aware of rustling sounds and soft female whispers somewhere above his head. Glancing up, he saw a finely wrought ivory screen edging a high balcony. Small slits were cut through the ivory, and Charles thought he caught a glint of light in an eye pressed to a hole in the screen. Seeing his glance, a courtier told the lieutenant that the wives and concubines of the mandarin were secreted behind the ivory screen, where they watched the strange white men who had come to their palace from a foreign land.

After protracted farewells, the naval officers exited the palace via the grand entryway. As Charles passed an elaborately painted screen, a hand reached out suddenly and plucked the blue-and-white-checkered bandana from his neck. Charles turned quickly and saw the edge of a silken robe disappear behind the screen. He shrugged off the theft and followed his fellow officers back to his ship.

The next day, a servant came aboard the battleship carrying a rice paper–wrapped package for Charles. When the lieutenant opened it, he found his checkered bandana covered on both sides with delicately embroidered flowers and birds. Charles put the bandana thoughtfully away in his inner pocket and went to the town to visit a certain fisherman who had befriended the Virginian when he first arrived in China. The old man examined the embroidered bandana closely and then told the lieutenant that it contained a message hidden in the embroidery, asking Charles to present himself at a certain side door of the mandarin's palace at a certain hour that night.

Upon so presenting himself, Charles was introduced to Flower of Love, the enchanting young wife of the aged mandarin. Flower of Love had seen the handsome blond officer through the enclosed balcony screen and had fallen for the man so exotic in looks, so much closer to her in age. Every night at the conclusion of his naval watch, Charles would knock on the secret door of the palace and follow a servant through a perfumed garden to a small summerhouse, where Flower of Love awaited him.

What started as a daring adventure became a love affair that consumed the lieutenant's mind and heart. Charles went about his duties like a man in a dream. Nothing was real to him save Flower of Love and her night garden. His naval duties—once the center of his world—became a nuisance, a boring way to pass the time until evening fell. Charles was almost mad with his longing for Flower of Love. He begged her to run away with him, to leave her aged husband and come to America. When she agreed, Charles booked passage for two on a merchant ship, prepared to flee China with the mandarin's lovely wife.

On the appointed evening, Charles packed his kit and stole away from the naval warship. After he entered the mandarin's palace through the secret door, he made his way through the night garden to the summerhouse. As he stepped inside, Charles was seized from behind and bound hand and foot. His captors thrust a gag into his mouth, carried him to the inner courtyard of the palace, and threw him down at the feet of the mandarin and his assembled household. Everyone was there—wives, children, servants, and soldiers.

Charles uttered not a word as he staggered to his feet, knowing that his fate was sealed. He squared his shoulders, determined to die like a man and an officer. A small smile fluttered briefly across the mandarin's lips when Charles met his gaze squarely. He lifted his fan and snapped it open, the sound echoing around the silent courtyard like a gunshot. At this signal, a parade of servants marched through a narrow archway, leading Flower of Love between them. She was dressed like a bride in white and silver, with pearls and flowers in her black hair. Her exquisite perfume filled the air as she entered the courtyard with dignity and faced her Virginian lover with a smile of gentle pride. Something in her face and bearing warned the lieutenant that something terrible faced him—perhaps something even worse than death, though he could not fathom what that might be.

Charles cried out through his gag when the servants seized the mandarin's unfaithful wife and tore off her bridal array before the silent eyes of his entire household. The soldiers seized Charles as he struggled to free himself and spring to the defense of the woman he loved. The servants grabbed the defenseless woman roughly by her bare arms and thrust her into the face of her American lover in the mockery of a kiss. Flower of Love was pressed so close to Charles that he could feel her warmth, smell her perfume, and see the love and resignation in her lovely dark eyes. Too soon, the servants pulled her away and stood her just out of arm's reach of her lover, facing her husband.

The mandarin stepped down from his throne and bowed to the American naval officer. Then he removed the silver dagger from the lieutenant's belt and saluted him with it in the American style. Turning swiftly toward Flower of Love, the mandarin raised the dagger. Charles screamed in horror against his gag. With one mighty thrust, the mandarin cleaved his faithless wife in two from head to toe, disemboweling her before the eyes of her American lover as her blood spurted out over his uniform. Charles stood transfixed with horror as the mandarin cut out her heart and threw her body at her lover's feet. With a second bow, the mandarin thrust the bloodstained silver knife back into Charles's belt and had the lieutenant dragged through the night garden and flung through the secret door where the love affair had first begun.

When Charles regained consciousness, he was aboard his naval vessel, which was already many leagues out to sea on its way home to Virginia. Charles left the service when he reached Virginia and never spoke of his time in the Orient except once, in private, to his older brother. But he kept the silver dagger and the embroidered bandana in remembrance of Flower of Love.

When his parents arranged a betrothal between Charles and a lovely Virginian heiress, he made no protest. Nothing mattered to him anymore. His world, his heart, was buried somewhere in China.

"Six weeks before the wedding," Grandfather concluded, "Charles, myself, and the heiress were riding along this ravine by the light of the full moon. She was a blonde beauty and a bit of a coquette. Wishing to prove her power over her swain, she pointed to this pine tree, leaning so precariously over the deep ravine, and said, 'Climb this tree, Charles. I dare you!' And Charles did."

I sat up abruptly, staring wide-eyed at my grandfather. "You mean the ghost of the falling man is my Uncle Charles?"

Grandfather nodded sadly. "I was there that night, when Charles climbed the tree. I saw the look on his face as he deliberately stepped on the rotten branch at the top. If you listen closely, you can hear his ghost calling his lover's name, Flower of Love, as he falls."

Elaine wept softly into Charlie's shoulder as he stroked her hair. I handed her the embroidered bandana, and she smiled at me through her tears.

"I thought *your* Charles should have a happy ending to his story," Grandfather said to my sister. He patted Elaine awkwardly on the shoulder and walked stiffly down the ravine path toward the house. I kissed her on the cheek and followed him, leaving the lovers alone in the light of a full moon.

Angel

I don't do battlefields—not because I am against history but because I'm psychic. I find battlefields, well, overwhelming is the best word I can come up with. Truth is, I don't deal at all well with being psychic, having been raised in a family of scientists and "seeing is believing" kind of people. I was the only one on either side of my family who had any sort of ESP, and it made things rather difficult growing up.

For instance, I didn't know until we moved out of our house when I was seven years old that the reclusive lady who lived in our attic room and spent all her days staring out the window was a ghost. Until I asked my mother about her on the day we left, I'd always believed we rented out the attic room to the pale lady in the long dress. Mom laughed at my "strange fantasies" and told me to stop making up stories. That's when I realized the woman I'd seen was a ghost—and that my practical family would probably not believe whatever I told them about her.

I was right. My parents had trouble explaining to themselves how I was able to pass them food a split second before they actually asked me to. And my brothers thought it was weird the way I always knew when one of them got hurt in football

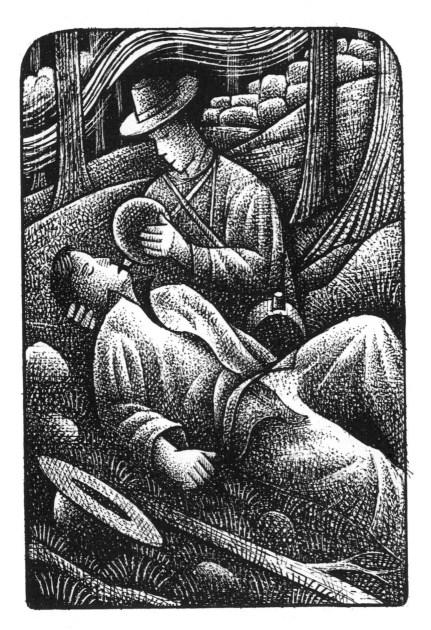

ANGEL

practice. But all of them figured there was some scientific explanation behind it. We had several difficult conversations along these lines before I gave up trying to explain my abilities to them.

Still, I thought it was kind of fun being psychic—until the day my friend Katie invited me to visit her house, which she claimed was haunted. Boy, was she right! And it wasn't a nice ghost. Katie's house was haunted by a murderer, and his spirit was very angry. I saw him as soon as I stepped inside the foyer. He was just a dark shadow looming up by the ceiling, and when he realized I could see him, he swooped down and tried to smother me. Choking for breath, I ran outside the house, trying to escape the dark spirit. As soon as I reached the front lawn, the spirit left me, forced back inside the house by whatever bound him there. That was the first time I realized how dangerous being psychic could be.

After that incident, I tried to shut down my "sixth sense," burying it deep beneath school work and after-school activities. I was mostly successful until my high school class took a trip to Gettysburg, Pennsylvania. I was so excited when I learned we were going to Gettysburg. The battle there was a turning point in the Civil War, and I'd read several historical novels about it in addition to the section in our school textbook.

As soon as I stepped out of the bus onto the battlefield, I was overwhelmed by the smells and sounds of battle. I staggered a few steps, dazed by the feelings of fear, pain, and death that bombarded me from all sides. The feelings overwhelmed me, and I fainted right at my teacher's feet. It was horrible, not to mention embarrassing. I couldn't explain to anyone what had happened. They wouldn't have believed me. So I pretended that I had the flu and spent the day lying down in the bus.

That was the first and last time I visited a battlefield. No way did I want to experience that again. Of course when I moved to Virginia with my new husband shortly after graduating from college, I knew it was going to be hard to avoid battlefields. And haunted houses, for that matter. Virginia was full of history, going all the way back to the Jamestown settlement and the wars between Indian tribes before that. And my new husband was a history buff—which made it all the more likely that I was going to be dragged off to one or more places that I'd find psychically uncomfortable.

Fortunately, my husband was a firm believer in psychic phenomena. He'd better be—his mother, Sylvia, was a white witch. She and I had bonded right from the start, and it was thanks to her that I was gradually coming to accept my psychic birthright.

When my husband suggested a day trip to Fredericksburg, I put him off until I had a chance to call my mama-in-law. She patiently listened to my fears and then suggested that I give it a try. I was much older now than I had been when I visited Gettysburg, and I'd spent nearly a year practicing the techniques she'd taught me for channeling and controlling my psychic abilities. This would be a good test for me.

We went to Fredericksburg on a sunny weekend in September. Fredericksburg was the scene of three major Civil War battles, but we decided to visit just one that day, since this was my very first "battlefield recovery trip," as my husband dubbed our excursion. We chose the Battle of Fredericksburg site, and my husband was careful to park our convertible under the shade of a big tree near the bookstore—just in case I needed to retreat there while he toured the battlefield and cemetery.

As soon as I stepped out of the car, I smelled gunpowder and sweat and just a hint of blood in the air. I took a deep breath and began a meditation ritual that Sylvia had taught me. The little ritual calmed my nerves, and my husband held my hand to keep me grounded in the present as we strolled to the visitor center.

First we watched a film about the battle to refresh our memories about the history of this place. According to the film, the Union Army of the Potomac—commanded by General Burnside—attacked Robert E. Lee's Confederate Army of Northern Virginia in a series of futile frontal assaults on December 13, 1862. The Union lost more than six thousand men, and the defeat brought the campaign against the Confederate capital of Richmond to an early end.

Watching the carnage from the center of his line, General Lee was quoted as saying, "It is well that war is so terrible, or we should grow too fond of it."

I was truly appalled by the loss of life on this battlefield. It was in a thoughtful frame of mind that we emerged from the film. As we headed toward the door, my husband gave me an inquiring look.

"Ready?" he asked.

"Ready," I replied, bracing my shoulders and giving him a brave grin. We set off into the warm sunshine to look at the re-creation of the stone wall beside the sunken road where Lee's army had successfully repulsed the Union forces on a foggy December day so long ago.

As we approached the stone wall, I shivered. The air felt cold and clammy, as though a fog had descended upon me. I clutched my husband's hand and blinked, trying to see the sunlight through the mist gathering before my eyes.

Breathe, I reminded myself. *Breathe.*

I could hear cannon firing from somewhere above me, and the sharp smell of gunfire filled my nostrils. I stopped for a moment, and my husband stopped with me. I felt his hand in mine, but could no longer see him. For a moment I felt the same panic that had overwhelmed me at Gettysburg. But my mama-in-law had told me to relax and go with it, so I took another deep breath and looked around me. And saw . . .

. . . a wide field covered with men's bodies where a moment before had been houses and trees. I saw a line of men in blue staggering futilely forward under heavy gunfire, barely able to get off a shot against the Confederates lined against them. Blood and smoke were everywhere. I gasped, and the scene disappeared . . .

I blinked in the sudden warmth and sunshine and found my husband watching me quizzically. "Okay?" he asked. I nodded, speechless, and allowed him to lead me along the paved walkway to the first of the signs explaining the battle.

I felt a little queasy when we stepped onto the sunken road, but it was not as bad as I had thought it would be. Just at the edge of my vision, I could see a shimmering as if two pictures—one from the past and one from the present—were trying to coexist in the same place. Suddenly, right in my ear I heard a male voice with a distinctly Southern accent shout "Fire!" I jumped. My husband squeezed my hand but didn't ask me to explain, for which I was thankful.

We were standing beside a white house next to the stone wall, looking in the windows to see one of the interior walls that still contained bullet holes from the battle, when the shimmering rose up around me again. I took a deep breath . . .

. . . and was suddenly conscious of a quaking fear deep in my gut and of a fierce resolution to do my duty, no matter what. I looked up and saw a wide expanse of field in front of me. I was pushing my way resolutely forward, holding my gun before me. I'd spent my bullet uselessly a moment ago and was trying to keep abreast of my comrades while I fumbled to reload.

Several hundred yards in front of me was a low stone wall, lined with a seemingly endless supply of blazing Confederate guns. Union soldiers—my brothers in arms—were falling all around me as bullets whizzed past. The combined smell of smoke, swampland, and gunpowder filled my nostrils, and my ears rang from the terrible blast of the cannon on the heights.

Then a horrible pain wrenched through my gut and I fell into the damp grass of the field, the world going misty and dark around me. Through bitter pain, I heard gunfire and heard the cries of the dying around me. But I couldn't move, couldn't help them; I couldn't help myself.

A long while later, the gunfire ceased except for an occasional blast. I was swimming through a sea of pain, conscious of nothing save a terrible thirst. I heard my own voice babbling, begging for water. It did not sound like me at all. Then I felt gentle hands lifting my head, and a canteen was against my parched lips. Cool water poured into my mouth, and I swallowed gratefully. I forced my eyes open and glanced up into the face of a young man in Confederate gray. "Thank you," I whispered hoarsely . . .

. . . I was back in the present, leaning with my head against the glass of the white house. My husband was rubbing my back, his face creased with concern.

"Honey," he said, shaking my shoulder gently. "I asked if you wanted to go back to the car."

I straightened up and looked at him, still dazed from the sharp memories of the past. After taking a moment to reground, I noticed that the faint sounds of battle had faded from the edges of my hearing and that the air had stopped shimmering. I sighed deeply. "I think it's over," I said tentatively, running a quick internal assessment of my "spooky" senses. Nothing; everything felt normal.

"Okay," he said after studying me for a long moment. "Ready to go on?"

I smiled a little tremulously. "Ready," I replied.

We headed down the path toward a monument standing a few yards from the house. My steps slowed as we approached, and I felt a lump rise in my throat. It pictured a man offering a canteen of water to a wounded soldier. I recognized the man immediately. I'd just seen him in my vision from the past.

I hurried closer, my pulses racing madly, and read his name: "Richard Rowland Kirkland." The carved writing on the monument continued: "At the risk of his life, the American soldier of sublime compassion brought water to his wounded foes at Fredericksburg. The fighting men on both sides of the line called him the Angel of Marye's Heights."

Tears filled my eyes. Yes, that's who I'd seen: the Angel of Marye's Heights. That same sixth sense that gave me visions of the past told me that this brave young soldier had not survived the war. He'd died on a distant battlefield, doing his duty for the Confederate States of America.

In that moment I realized I was done, physically and emotionally.

"Honey, I'd like to go back to the car," I said.

My husband took one look at my tear-stained face and agreed. He tucked me into the front seat of the convertible and put the top down so that I could enjoy the balmy day. Snuggled under a light summer blanket, I poured myself some tea out of a thermos we'd prepared at my mama-in-law's suggestion. My husband went on to tour the rest of the battlefield while I rested and pondered my experiences.

I'd done pretty well, I decided; not bad for my first time out. And I had a young soldier to look up in the history books when I got home. Or when my husband came back, maybe we could find a book about him in the park gift shop.

I sighed and snuggled under the blanket. *Who knows,* I thought as I settled down for a nap. *Maybe next week we can visit Chancellorsville. Maybe.*

12

The Horseman

BOWLING GREEN

When my husband of forty years died, leaving me penniless and alone, the Colonel—who was a distant cousin—and his wife took me in. I was going to help mind the Colonel's young sons and would act as a companion to his wife.

The Colonel and his family lived in a mansion that was so fancy it made my head spin. It seemed strange to be living in such luxury after being so poor all my life. But fate is strange sometimes.

The day I arrived at the mansion, I noticed the old box hedge by the house. For some reason, I was nearly frozen with terror the first time I saw it. It felt as though a goose were walking over my grave, as my granny used to say. The shadows seemed darker there than any other place on the property.

When darkness fell that night, I saw five ghost lights appear one by one over the hedge and float down to hover just above the ground below it. The lights were evenly spaced about eight to ten feet apart. The hair stood up on my neck when I saw them.

When I mentioned what I'd seen at dinner that night, the Colonel told me the whole thing was just silly superstition. He was quite cross with me, and I was not surprised when his wife

THE HORSEMAN

told me afterward that it was best not to mention superstitions around the Colonel. I thanked her for her good advice, and we let the matter drop. But I knew that something wasn't right about that hedge and vowed to avoid the place as much as I could.

It soon became apparent that the Colonel went far beyond merely disliking superstitions. He took a perverse delight in poking fun at those among his family and friends who believed in ghosts, omens, and bad luck. At dinner the evening after I reported seeing the ghost lights, he solemnly presented me with a bouquet of branches from the box hedge. Having taken the Colonel's measure, I thanked him politely and asked the serving maid for a vase to put them in. I even insisted that the "bouquet" be placed on the table as a centerpiece during our meal, which made the children giggle. Even the Colonel laughed when he saw how funny it looked, and I knew he'd decided I was all right, despite the inauspicious beginning of our relationship.

I was not the only one that the Colonel teased. I quickly discovered that there were a number of cats running around the grounds of the mansion—all of them black. And I found a mirror with a single crack in it that hung in a remote corner near the back entrance. About two weeks after I moved to the mansion, I found a garden path that contained an ivy-covered ladder artfully hung between two trees so that anyone using the path had to walk underneath it. I laughed when I saw it, appreciating the Colonel's subtle humor.

But my favorite joke took place nightly in the dining parlor, which was always set for thirteen people, no matter how many were actually dining there. The uneven table setting made visitors uneasy without quite knowing why. Only the most observant thought to count the number of place settings, and I saw more than one of the Colonel's guests turn a little green when they realized they were sitting at a table set for thirteen!

One night about a month after I arrived at the mansion, the Colonel and his wife were entertaining several out-of-town guests at their table. Suddenly our meal was interrupted by the sound of pounding hooves galloping around the track in front of the house. The approach of the horseman sounded so urgent that all of us at the table rose and hurried to the front door to see what was wrong. But when the Colonel opened the door, there was no horseman galloping madly through the twilight. The track and the front garden were empty save for a group of four or five children playing on the grass down near the gate to the road. It was hard to make them out in the dim light, but I thought it looked like young boys playing with a ball.

Puzzled by the strange occurrence, we went back to our meal and a lively debate took place as to the meaning of what we'd all heard. The Colonel maintained that the horseman had merely ridden around the house before we got to the door, but that seemed unlikely to me. He'd have had to been riding very fast indeed to disappear around the house before the door was opened, and surely we would have heard the horse's hooves pounding so hard in the grass.

The mystery was driven forcibly out of our heads the next day when the Colonel's eldest boy took sick—very sick. His fever was so high that he went into convulsions and died before nightfall. Oh, it was sad! I'd already grown to love the boys as my own, and to lose one so suddenly was a terrible tragedy.

It wasn't until the Colonel announced that they were going to bury the boy under the box hedge by the house that

I remembered the ghost lights I'd seen there. I went very still, and my eyes went to my cousin's wife to see if she recalled the vision I'd had when I first arrived. But she had forgotten, for which I was grateful. I kept remembering how I'd seen five lights appearing one after another, evenly spaced along the hedge. Almost like grave markers . . . No! It was nonsense. I turned away from my thoughts with a shudder and went to comfort the little boys in the nursery. But I couldn't help thinking that the Colonel had five sons . . .

Things gradually returned to normal at the mansion, and my new life settled into an enjoyable routine filled with romps with the boys, quiet walks in the garden with my cousin's wife, and intellectual debates with the Colonel over the chessboard at night. I became one of the family and the boys started calling me "Grandmamma," a nickname that was quickly adopted by everyone at the mansion, including the Colonel and his wife. I was everyone's confidant, and sometimes Cook would let me into the kitchen to bake my secret cookie recipe, which brought extravagant praise from the Colonel whenever I made them.

Life was sweet, and I was not prepared when—almost a year to the day after we first heard it—the phantom horseman again came galloping up the road and into the track in front of the house. Only the family was dining at the mansion that night. The Colonel and his lady both turned pale when they heard the sound, so like that of the previous year. I sprang up with dread and hurried toward the front door, the Colonel and his wife at my heels. I pulled the door open and in the dim twilight looked out onto an empty track. Down by the front gate, I saw the same group of children playing together on the grass—boys, every one of them. And for a moment I thought one of them looked like the Colonel's eldest son!

The Colonel ushered us back inside and firmly closed the door as if nothing was wrong. But we all felt uneasy, remembering what had happened the day after the phantom horseman had been heard on the track.

"Nonsense," the Colonel said aloud, voicing what I was too shy to say. It had to be a coincidence. Still, I gave all the boys an extra hard hug before bed that night, afraid to speak lest my words caused something terrible to happen. Fortunately the boys all appeared happy and healthy and full of mischief at breakfast the next morning. It wasn't until late in the afternoon that the Colonel's second eldest son was accidentally kicked in the head by one of the horses out by the stable. He died instantly.

The Colonel's wife and I were convinced that the horseman and the children by the gate were not a coincidence. They were harbingers of death. The Colonel was furious with us for voicing our theory. He stormed out of the house and went to the neighbors to inquire if their children had been out last night when the children had appeared at the gate. But all of the neighborhood children were home eating dinner with their families at the time the apparition had appeared. And—though I didn't say it—I still thought one of the children by the front gate had been the Colonel's eldest son.

The second boy was buried under the box hedge beside his brother. I noted with sinking heart that his grave was in the place where I'd seen the second ghost light on my first day at the mansion.

We kept a careful watch on the three remaining sons that year. The boys were high spirited and a bit resentful of the extra restrictions, but we didn't want to lose another child to illness or an accident. And every night at dinner we listened for the phantom horseman. Thankfully, he did not come.

When the anniversary of the boys' deaths passed without incident, we all relaxed our vigil and the unspoken tension at dinner abated, which made the third arrival of the horseman all the more terrible. It happened a week later, at exactly the same time as the first two visitations. Dinner was almost over when we heard the horseman galloping at great speed up the road and into the track in front of the house. By the time we got to the door, the horseman was nowhere to be seen. But the phantom children were there again, playing by the gate. And two of the boys appeared strikingly like the Colonel's two eldest children.

The Colonel gave a shout and ran down the lawn toward the children, but they vanished into the twilight before he made it halfway down the track. Beside me, the Colonel's wife moaned and raced upstairs to the nursery to clutch her little son to her bosom, afraid to let him out of her sight lest something dreadful occurred. When I came downstairs after tucking them both into a rocking chair with soothing words and a blanket, I found the Colonel slumped into his favorite chair in the study. "Grandmamma," he said without looking up, "Grandmamma."

He sounded as lost and alone as a little boy, and I gave him a hug. What else could I do? What else could I say? There were five ghost lights by the hedge, and the Colonel had five sons . . .

The third little boy died in his mama's arms that night from a sudden seizure. It happened so quickly that there was no time to go for the doctor. We heard her screaming frantically from the nursery and came running. The poor mite was writhing in a desperate attempt to breathe. We shook him to expel anything lodged in his throat, but there was nothing blocking it. We ran down to the kitchen and tried to open his lungs with a steam bath, but it didn't work. He died a few minutes later in his mother's arms. Asthma, the doctor called it when he examined the poor little body the next morning. He told us that there wasn't anything we could have done to save him—small comfort when faced with the loss of a third child.

Now there were three little bodies buried beneath the box hedge, and the Colonel and his wife lived in constant fear for their two remaining sons. Anytime we heard a horseman passing on the road or riding up the track I would run to the window or door to look. And I know my cousin's wife did the same. As for the Colonel, his whole attitude toward superstitions had changed after the death of his third son. He got rid of all the black cats roaming the property. He put an unbroken mirror in the back hallway. He took the ladder down from over the path in the garden. And he stopped setting the dinner table for thirteen.

This new philosophy of the Colonel seemed to help, for we were spared another tragedy for several years. As time wore on, the memory of the phantom horseman faded a little, and our fears faded with it. But always, in the back of my mind, I saw five ghost lights hovering under the box hedge. Five, not three . . .

By this time, my age had caught up with me. I couldn't romp with the boys anymore. And really, they were getting too big for little-boy games. I was so proud of them. They liked to sit by my rocking chair and tell me stories and read to me. I was almost crippled with rheumatism, but their stories made me feel young again.

When we heard the phantom horseman the fourth time, I was in too much pain from the rheumatism to get up out of my chair and peer out the front door with the Colonel. But it didn't matter. I knew what he saw: A group of young boys playing by the front gate. I wondered if he recognized his three sons. The next day the fourth son died in a carriage accident.

I was an old, old woman when the horseman arrived for the fifth son. I thought maybe I would be the fifth ghost light and spare the Colonel and his lady this final tragedy. Death was creeping nearer every day. I could feel it in my bones. But the horseman had not come for me. He had come to take my last beloved boy away.

When I heard the phantom galloping up the track, I was too sad to cry. We didn't tell the boy that the horseman had come. How can you tell a beloved child that he is doomed? But he didn't seem surprised when the same illness that had struck down his eldest brother befell him suddenly the next day. He just asked to sit with his Grandmamma in her rocking chair as his fever raged out of control. An hour later, he died in my arms, and I knew that he would be buried beside his brothers under the box hedge.

I looked over his head into the face of his weary, grieving mother and I said: "I'll look after all the boys for you, my dear. We will wait for you to come home."

Fighting her tears she whispered, "I know you will, Grandmamma. I know you will."

"The horseman won't come again," I told the Colonel as he lifted his dead son out of my weary arms.

"I know, Grandmamma," the Colonel said tenderly through his tears. "You rest now."

So I closed my eyes and let the darkness fall over me. I was so tired. Five ghost lights. Five graves. Five little boys playing by the front gate.

My head fell forward and I breathed my last.

At the end of a long tunnel, I saw a beautiful light. Waiting there for me was my husband, and beside him stood five mischievous little boys.

"Grandmamma," shouted the youngest joyfully. All five boys ran to meet me, and with joyful laughter they pulled me deeper into the light and into my husband's waiting arms.

13

Phantasie

JAMESTOWN

The cursed tree fell the wrong way at the wrong moment. And there I was, laid up with a busted leg just a day before Captain Smith left on his exploration mission. That meant I was left too—left behind, that is. My good wife tried to console me, but I was mad as hornets at missing out on the danger and excitement that always filled the Captain's missions.

"He will tell thee all about it when he returns," she said soothingly, wiping my fevered brow with a damp cloth. "Do not fret so, my love."

Easy for her to say. She liked staying home to tend to the farm work and gossip with the other ladies in the settlement. But I was born with wanderlust, and the Captain's explorations suited my temperament far better than being housebound.

Time dragged slowly while I was laid up. Things got a little better once my leg was pronounced whole again and I could be up and about the normal farm chores and other doings in the settlement. I kept myself busy, but I always had half an ear open for the Captain. When I heard the first shouts heralding the return of the explorers a few months later, I raced off to

PHANTASIE

greet them. The Captain gave a wry smile when he saw me and commented laughingly on my recovery.

"Next time I'll stay away from trees," I promised him with a grin. "How did you fare?"

"We saw many things of interest," Captain Smith told me. "I have much to tell you, my friend, including a strange tale related to me while we were abroad."

"Come to dinner tomorrow," I said. "My wife will be glad to see you. You can tell us both your tale then."

The Captain accepted my dinner invitation with pleasure and proceeded to his own dwelling to wash off the weeks of grime and see to the paperwork that awaited him. The next evening found him eating ravenously of my good wife's cooking as he told us of his latest adventures in the wilds surrounding our small colony. The Captain was a dynamic man with a charisma that endeared him to many. When he told a story, you could think of nothing else until the tale was finished. We gasped and shuddered at the scary bits and laughed ourselves silly over the jests. In short, we were the perfect audience for the Captain.

He did not bring up the "strange tale" until we were seated comfortably around the fireplace in the parlor, sipping tea and eating the cake my wife had made for our dessert. The winter days were short, and it was already dusk outside. The glow from the fire was a welcome light.

I watched the Captain's bearded face grow sober. To my surprise, this hard and fearless man looked almost frightened for a moment. He caught my eye upon him and smiled in a self-deprecating manner.

"We met with a great Indian chief during our journey," he began, his eyes on the flickering fire in front of us. "He had lost many of his people in a rather short period of time, and the tale he told of that loss has kept me awake on more nights than I'd admit to."

He glanced up at me as he spoke, and I nodded in understanding. The Captain had a larger-than-life air about him that had carried him through some troubled times, both in England and in the New World. He carefully protected the reputation he'd developed as a bold and fearless man, and very few were allowed to see behind that mask to the vulnerable person underneath. My wife and I were two of the privileged few.

Reassured of our support—and our silence on this matter— the Captain told the following story.

In the Indian village lived a man and his wife who married late. For many years they had no children, which distressed them greatly. Then, one after another, the wife gave birth to two boys. The whole village rejoiced with the couple, and the little lads grew strong and brave. They were handsome of face and charming of manner and quickly became favorites with everyone.

Then tragedy struck. Some childhood sickness overcame the younger, and soon both boys were ill; they died soon after. The whole village was heartbroken; but none more so than the parents, who mourned until they were so thin and ill that the chief feared for their lives.

The bodies of the two boys were carefully dressed and laid side by side on a narrow board that their dazed father constructed for them. The grieving parents refused to bury their children, not wishing to consign their beloved sons into the cold earth. Day followed day, and the mother gazed longingly upon her dead sons, hoping and wishing passionately for their return.

One day she came running into the center of the village, her wan cheeks flushed with excitement. The boys were coming back, she exclaimed to one and all. Their dead bodies had once again assumed the flush of youth and vitality, and she was sure they would awaken soon and be as they once were.

Her doubting husband came running at once to see, followed by all who heard her words. And it was just as the mother had proclaimed. The boys lay as if sleeping, their faces once more glowing with health and vitality. They seemed almost incandescent, as if lit from within. Anyone who gazed upon them had difficulty looking away, and the eyes of those who looked upon the apparent miracle began to glow with that same strange incandescence.

The report came swiftly to the ears of the village medicine man. He shuddered when he heard it, and for a moment he felt as though a great black cloud covered his face, suffocating him. The air grew cold and he gasped, raising his hands to swat away the blackness before his eyes. The woman who brought the news was so frightened by the medicine man's reaction that she fled from his home in distress.

The medicine man grabbed hold of his medicine bag and prayed until the darkness and cold sensations left him. He shook from head to toe in fear. He did not want to see this so-called miracle. He did not want to gaze upon the countenances of the dead children. He knew instinctively that there was evil afoot. Such a black omen could not be easily dismissed. Still, because his chief was away at the moment, it was his duty to investigate the apparent miracle.

With heavy heart, the medicine man made his way to the place where the two corpses lay in their funeral finery. And it was just as the woman had described. The boys' bodies were glowing from within, and a semblance of their previous health and vitality was on their faces. The medicine man shuddered and turned away after one quick glance. Could this truly be a working of the spirits? Or was it some evil phantasie meant to harm his people? Deeply troubled, the medicine man withdrew to fast and pray, hoping the spirits would give him an answer.

Meanwhile, word of the miracle was spreading through the village. Many came to look upon the boys, and all who saw them turned away with the same strange glow in their eyes that marked the faces of the dead. The mother hovered over her children, overjoyed by what she saw, while the father spread the word abroad. Their sons were returning to them, climbing the spirit path from death to life, and soon they would be restored completely.

Deeply frightened, the medicine man tried to stop people from going to witness the "miracle." But the people did not heed his warning. They continued to crowd around the dead bodies and stare at them in dazzled fascination.

Suddenly the miracle ceased as rapidly as it had begun. The glow of health and vitality seeped away from the countenance of the dead boys, and they were once again empty carcasses, rotting slowly away beneath their funeral finery. With a cry of agony, the mother collapsed and fell ill. The medicine man, called to tend her, saw that her eyes still retained the faint glow they'd developed when she looked upon the phantasie covering the faces of her sons.

By the time the chief returned from his trip, the mother was dead and her husband was dying. And he was not the only one ill. All the villagers who had gazed upon the "miracle" were suffering from a strange sickness that did not respond to any of the medicine man's remedies. He was exhausted from trying to succor the ill, all of whom bore the mark of the phantasie in their eyes.

Soon everyone who could be spared was tending to the ill, but one by one, the villagers were dying. So many died so quickly that there was no time to bury them all. In the end, everyone who saw the "miracle" perished. Even the medicine man, who had gazed but briefly upon the dead boys, succumbed to the sickness. Only the great chief and those of his people who were away or busy during the hours that the phantasie fell upon the two corpses were spared.

The Captain's voice fell silent, and he rubbed a hand across his eyes as if to blot out the face of the great chief who had lost so many. He turned his gaze at last from the fire and smiled sadly at my wife and myself. "I do not know why this particular story should so disturb me. We have heard of ghosts and evil spirits before."

But I knew why. I could see in my mind's eye a picture of two rotting corpses, glowing from within as the eyes of the dazzled men and women beheld a phantasie of health and well-being. It made chills run up and down my spine. My wife gripped my hand tightly, and I knew she could picture it as well.

"Harbinger," she whispered. "It was a death omen."

I shook my head. "If it was an omen, why did it affect only the people who gazed upon the bodies? I think it was a demon."

"Whatever it was, it was certainly evil," Captain Smith said heavily. "I hope such a thing never visits the colony."

"At least we have been warned," I said. "If it does come here, we know what to do."

"Or not do," my wife corrected. She shuddered and hitched her chair closer to the fire. "Come, I've heard enough dark talk for one day. Let us speak of pleasant things."

The Captain smiled at her and agreed.

I went to bed in a fearful mood that night. In my mind, I could picture men and women walking around a distant village with a terrible incandescent glow in their eyes—a death glow. As I blew out the candle and settled next to my wife in bed, I sent up a prayer for those poor Indian villagers. Pray God they would never again be visited by such evil. And pray God it would never come here. Amen.

14

Old 97

They gave him his orders in Monroe, Virginia.

"Steve," the boss called from the office. "Old 97 is running an hour late. Get her into Spencer on time."

"Right boss," Steve Broady called as he joined his crew on the platform that fateful day in September 1903.

He hadn't been with Southern Railroad very long, but Broady already knew that time was money to the railroad. Old 97 was one of the fast trains under contract to the U.S. Postal Service. She ran the mail from Washington, D.C., to Atlanta, Georgia, earning $140,000 a year for her company. When she was on time. For every minute she was late, the railroad would forfeit some of that money to the Postal Service. An hour behind was a substantial chunk of change to lose in one go. This wouldn't look good to the big bosses, and it didn't matter to them that he was getting the locomotive and four cars—two mail, two luggage—nearly an hour behind schedule.

Riding the rails is a tough business, Broady thought as Old 97 steamed her way to a stop at the station. She was a beauty. Broady paused for a brief second to admire the ten-wheel engine that had been born in the Baldwin Locomotive Works.

OLD 97

She could maintain an average speed of forty miles an hour and had a reputation for always running on time. This delay was unusual.

The main crew had been transferred to another train at Monroe, so they exited the locomotive and handed her over to Broady and his team. One old-timer stopped beside the engineer and said, "Bad news, mate. We've got a load of live canaries on board today. You be careful."

Canaries were supposed to be bad luck on the rails. Broady felt a shudder run up his spine, and his hands suddenly felt cold and sweaty at the same time. He didn't need any bad luck on the train, not with so much time to make up.

He thanked the old-timer and then settled in the locomotive and made sure everything was ready to roll. The time allotted for this particular run—Monroe to Spencer—was four hours and fifteen minutes. To do this, Old 97 had to average about thirty-nine miles per hour. But if he was to make up that extra hour for Southern . . .

Steve Broady did some quick calculations and whistled under his breath. He'd have to run the train at fifty-one miles per hour to do it. And this was tricky terrain, full of steep hills, deep valleys, and sharp curves. He could feel the firemen's eyes on him as he pulled out of the station. Both of them knew what it would take to get back on schedule. He'd be whittling to beat the band. Whittling was railroad parlance for going full throttle on the straight stretches and braking just enough to safely make the curves. It was dangerous, and engineers weren't supposed to do it. But the railroad turned a blind eye when money was involved.

It wouldn't be easy, but Broady meant to try. He picked up speed as soon as they were clear of the station and opened the throttle. Thirty miles an hour. Forty miles an hour. Then fifty. They were flying!

The countryside became a blur of greens and grays and browns as Old 97 screamed her way down the tracks toward Spencer. Broady had been instructed to skip one of the intermediary stops to gain time, so he blew right through Franklin Junction. And his pause in Lynchburg was so brief that a young fellow sent onto Old 97 to check the locks on the safe was stranded aboard the train.

Broady slowed for the worst of the curves but kept the throttle open as much as he could. They were gaining time with every mile, and Steve was beginning to relax a bit, sure that they would make Spencer on or very close to on time. Then he realized they were closing in on Danville. Old 97 was heading into a three-mile downgrade. The steep hill had a nasty curve leading onto the Stillhouse Trestle, a seventy-five-foot-high bridge spanning the creek. Signs warned engineers to take the trestle curve at fifteen miles per hour, and he was going nearly fifty! Broady reached for the air brake—and got nothing. He'd been whittling the train so fast he'd used up the steam and air pressure faster than the compressors could make it. Old 97 had no brakes!

Broady threw the engine in reverse in a desperate attempt to lock the wheels, hoping that would slow the train down enough to make the tight curve ahead. As he did, he sounded the whistle to alert the men in the other cars to throw on the hand brakes because the train was a "wildcat," railroad parlance for a runaway.

"Please, God," Broady prayed as the whistle screamed its shrill message. "Please!"

Old 97 roared straight at the curve, whistle screaming. Broady's whole body braced in terror as chills ran all over his skin. Then time seemed to slow as the train jumped the rails, going in a straight line where it should have curved with the trestle. The flange on the engine wheels broke; the locomotive grazed a telegraph pole and ripped through the wires running parallel to the tracks. Then the tender was soaring through the air, followed by its four cars. For a split second, the train was parallel to the ground. Then gravity kicked in and Old 97 plunged seventy-five feet into the chasm beneath the trestle bridge, the whistle screaming as it fell.

The engine smashed into the creek at the bottom of the ravine with a terrific boom and plunged deep into the water and mud, its drive wheels still turning. Scalding-hot steam cascaded out in every direction—killing most of the crew instantly— as the four cars that followed the engine smashed into it and one another. The ravine was filled with the horrible screech of crushing metal and the roar and hiss of escaping steam. The fourth and final car shuddered to a halt with one end pointing straight up at the sky. For an instant there was an awful silence. Then the air was filled with the shrill cries of released canaries fleeing from the wrecked train, followed by the alarmed shouts of Danville residents as rescuers and onlookers came running to the wreck.

Rescuers found Broady and the two firemen near the locomotive. All three were scalded almost beyond recognition, and the firemen were dead. Broady was lying in the creek, still horribly alive when the first men arrived. When a rescuer tried to pull him out, the engineer's skin peeled away from his poor burned body. He died a moment later; his watch had stopped at exactly 2:18 p.m.

Nine of the sixteen people on board Old 97 perished in the wreck, including Broady and the young man who'd been inadvertently caught aboard the train in Lynchburg. The railroad placed the blame for the crash squarely on Broady, but the official inquest said that while the cause of the wreck was obviously excessive speed, they could not determine whether it was equipment failure or the engineer that was to blame.

For many years following the wreck of Old 97, ghost lights appeared in the gorge at night, moving along the bank of the creek as if they were rescue lanterns searching for survivors. The lights continued to appear long after the railroad shifted its course and the Stillhouse Trestle was removed from the gorge.

And if you stand at the foot of the old three-mile downgrade just a little after 2:00 p.m. on autumn afternoons, folks say you can still hear the whistle of the runaway Old 97 as she tries yet again to finish her fateful run into Danville.

15

Bunny Man Bridge

CLIFTON

Growing up, I'd heard all kinds of stories about the Bunny Man, and I considered it complete nonsense. Still, when my buddies from birth—identical twin boys who lived next door—came over to tell ghost stories on Halloween night, it seemed natural to recount the tales we'd heard about our local legend, the Bunny Man.

The most commonly told story was about an insane killer who escaped from a local asylum in D.C. with his buddy and went into hiding in the woods near Clifton. Soon after the escape, local residents began finding skinned corpses of dismembered rabbits hanging from trees in the vicinity and in one memorable incident, from the tunnel under the railroad bridge. They reported the incidents to the police, but the authorities could not track down the person or persons responsible.

Then the escaped prisoners had a fight of some kind. The loser ended up gutted, skinned, and hung from the railroad bridge, just like the rabbits. A message nailed to his foot said, "You'll never find me, no matter how hard you try! [Signed] The Bunny Man."

BUNNY MAN BRIDGE

The residents of Clifton were scared out of their wits. The police were called in to investigate, but the Bunny Man continued to evade the authorities. All they could find were the grisly remains of rabbits hung mockingly from trees to show where the killer had been.

Then a local costume shop was broken into. The only thing stolen was a man-size costume of a white bunny. The owner of the store found a note written in rabbit's blood thrust onto the hanger where the costume had hung. It said: "Thanks for the suit. [Signed] The Bunny Man."

After the theft, people started seeing a white-clad figure running through the woods around Clifton. Parents grew frightened and kept their children in their own yards for fear of what the Bunny Man might do to them. The local police were hammered with complaints about the insane killer roaming the woods in a bunny suit, but they still could not capture the Bunny Man.

One night, a couple of teenage boys got drunk and boasted to their friends that they could find the Bunny Man, even if the police couldn't. Everyone laughed—until the boys didn't show up for school the next day. Their frantic parents called the police, who went in search of the missing boys. It didn't take long for them to locate the teens. They'd found the Bunny Man, all right, or he had found them. The police found their bodies hanging from the old railroad bridge, gutted and skinned just like the rabbits.

A huge manhunt was initiated, and the police finally spotted the Bunny Man lurking near the railroad bridge. When he realized he was trapped, the deranged man—still dressed in a huge white bunny suit—threw himself under the wheels of an oncoming train and was killed instantly.

Since then, it is said that the ghost of the Bunny Man haunts the old railroad bridge and that people foolish enough to cross the tracks at midnight won't live to see a new day.

Anyway, that's how the story goes. From my point of view, it was all hogwash. I didn't believe in ghosts. The Bunny Man was an urban legend—nothing to be scared about.

The twins, on the other hand, completely believed in the ghost of the Bunny Man.

"We should go to Bunny Man Bridge!" they said with gleams in their identical blue eyes. "It's the perfect place to be on Halloween night."

Yeah, right. Like I wanted to sit in the woods at midnight, waiting to see if the ghost of a deranged killer in a white bunny suit showed up to murder me.

"Not a chance," I said. "You're the ones who are crazy if you believe in that nonsense."

"Come on. It's Halloween. Don't you want a good scare?" they asked me.

"I'm busy," I said. "Cheryl asked me to come to her Halloween party."

"Ohhh! Cheryl!" The twins grinned at each other knowingly. They were so immature sometimes.

"Yeah, Cheryl," I growled. "Now get out of here so I can get ready for the party."

The twins were still talking about visiting the Bunny Man Bridge when they left my house. I felt a bit uneasy about that. The story of those two missing teens had gotten under my skin, but I shrugged it off. It was an urban legend, for goodness sake. Kids probably gathered at the Bunny Man Bridge every Halloween, and the police were all over it—nothing to worry about.

I went to Cheryl's Halloween party dressed as a swashbuckling pirate and danced with her the whole night. The party went on until midnight, when the parents of the nondrivers came to pick up their partygoers.

I didn't think any more about the twins until the next morning, when their mother phoned to ask if they'd slept over at my house. Apparently no one had seen the boys after they'd left our house last night, and their beds hadn't been slept in. I told the boys' mom that they had been talking about visiting the Bunny Man Bridge at midnight to see the ghost. "Maybe they're still there," I said, trying to ignore the knot in my gut.

We took a ride out to Bunny Man Bridge to see if the twins had gone there last night. *They probably fell asleep waiting to see the ghost,* I thought, shaking off the chills running up and down my arms. Stupid prank!

The drive seemed to take a long time. No one said much as we approached the tunnel under the railroad tracks. From our side, it looked empty. Or was it? My dad stopped the car abruptly, and we peered through the tunnel. On the far side we could see two pairs of legs hanging down from the tunnel entrance.

"Oh, dear God," gasped the twins' mother. We leapt out of the car and raced through the tunnel—and stopped in horror at the grisly scene. The twins' bloodstained bodies were hanging from the edge of the tunnel, twisting gently in the wind. The boys had been gutted and skinned like rabbits. And pinned to one foot was a note that read, "You'll never catch me! [Signed] The Bunny Man."

Hold Him, Tabb

HAMPTON

"Yep, I remember what it was like before the railroad came through these parts," Uncle Jeter reminisced, tapping the stem of his pipe against his cheek as he relaxed into the most comfortable chair by the fire.

I was sitting on a stool right next to the fireplace, occasionally throwing on another log, impatient for him to continue. Uncle Jeter told the best stories about the old days, but he wouldn't be rushed. I knew from previous experience that if I tried to hurry him, he would clam up and refuse to tell any stories at all. So I just waited, trying not to fidget.

"Back in those days, Matthew my boy, men had to be tough. I used to earn my living by carting supplies from town to town on horse-drawn wagons. Not easy work, no sir. Especially in winter."

Uncle Jeter paused to light his pipe with a small stick he took from the fireplace.

"One cold December day," he continued after the pipe was lit to his satisfaction, "I was traveling together with a number of wagons. About the middle of the afternoon it began to snow. We decided mighty quick that we should stop somewhere and

HOLD HIM, TABB

wait until morning to continue on. Old Ned, the tinsmith, he was the one who spotted an abandoned settlement near the roadside. It looked like a good place to ride out the storm. There was an old house and a barn with plenty of stalls for all our horses."

Uncle Jeter paused for a moment and shook his head. "We thought we were real lucky, finding such a good shelter. We were just about through unhitching the horses from the wagons when a fellow stopped by to talk to us. Claimed he was the owner of the property. Told us we were welcome to stay but the house was haunted. 'Haunted?' Tabb, a tinker traveling with us, asked. 'What do you mean haunted?' The owner said that no one who had ever stayed in that house had made it out alive, not for the last twenty-five years. That was good enough for me. I hitched Ol' Betsy back up to the wagon and moved up the road about half a mile to where a stand of trees offered some shelter from the snow. Everyone else followed me, except for Tabb. He thought we were plumb foolish and said so. He wasn't afraid of no ghosts, and he didn't plan on perishing in the snow with the rest of us.

"I was real uneasy about that, but I wasn't about to risk my neck in a haunted house. I stayed next to the road, though. I could see that Tabb had settled into the house nice and comfy, 'cause there was a light in the window and I saw smoke coming from the chimney. The rest of us built a fire as best we could and huddled together for warmth through the long night. I wondered a couple of times if Tabb wasn't the smart one and we the foolish. But the owner of the settlement had looked like an honest fellow, and he seemed right scared of that house, so I figured there must be something to it."

Uncle Jeter was so involved in his story now that he let his pipe go out.

"So what happened?" I asked.

"Well, just about dawn, I gave up trying to sleep and went back down the road to see how Tabb had fared for the night. I didn't go into the house, but I did peek through the windows on the first floor. When I got round the back, I saw Tabb snoozing peacefully in a big bed. He looked warm and happy. Then I saw a movement on the ceiling. I looked up, and there was a large man dressed all in white, floating flat against the ceiling. The man was right over Tabb, looking down on him. Scared me out of my wits.

"'Tabb,' I hissed, tapping at the window. 'Tabb, get out of there, you fool!'

"Tabb woke up at once, but instead of looking toward the window, he looked straight up and saw the man in white on the ceiling. Tabb gave an awful yell, but before he could move out of bed, that man fell down off the ceiling and landed right on top of him. Now Tabb was a big, strong fellow, but that ghost was powerful, and Tabb couldn't get the ghost to let him go. They wrestled back and forth on the bed. Sometimes Tabb would be on top and sometimes the ghost. I gave a shout and smashed the glass in the window, shouting, 'Hold him, Tabb, hold him!'

"'You can bet yer soul I've got him,' Tabb panted as he and the ghost fell off the bed.

"I could hear shouts behind me as I started to crawl in the window. The other wagoneers had heard the commotion and came to see what was wrong. Just then, the ghost flung himself and Tabb right at me, knocking me back out of the window and into the snow. The ghost levitated himself and Tabb right up onto the roof of the front porch. We all ran around the house to get a better view, shouting, 'Hold him, Tabb. Hold him!' The ghost and Tabb were wrestling frantically in the snow on the porch roof.

"'You can bet yer life I've got him,' gasped Tabb.

"The ghost gave a mighty leap and threw Tabb onto the roof of the house.

"'Hold him, Tabb!' I shouted with the other men. 'Hold him!'

"'You can bet yer boots I've got him,' Tabb yelled as he and the ghost tumbled over and over on the roof. Snow was pouring off the roof on all sides as they struggled. And then the ghost lifted Tabb right into the air.

"'Hold him, Tabb!' old Ned shouted. 'Hold him!' The rest of us were silent.

"'I got him,' Tabb cried. 'But he's got me too!'

"They were floating a few feet off the roof, still grappling with each other. And then the ghost carried Tabb straight up into the air. We watched them until they were both out of sight."

Uncle Jeter slowly leaned back into his chair.

"What happened to Tabb?" I cried. Uncle Jeter shook his head.

"None of us ever saw Tabb again," he said, and he refused to say another word for the rest of the evening.

17

The Haunted Tower

My Great-Uncle Powhatan was once a colonel in the Confederate army, until he was injured in battle in 1864. "Uncle Pow was shot in the head," Mama told my twin brother, Frank, and me when we were little. "His mother nursed him right here on the plantation. She brought him through alive when everyone thought he was dead, but when he woke from his coma, he had no memory of his life before. He didn't even know his own mother. The head injury left him a bit simple, so you must be very kind to old Uncle Pow."

Uncle Pow told the best stories in the world, and he was stronger than a team of oxen. He towered over us—six feet six inches in his bare feet—and loved to swing us around. He never remembered much of what happened on any given day, but that never bothered us. The adults treated Uncle Pow as if he were touched in the head. But to Frank and me, Uncle Pow was a war hero, and we were immensely proud of him.

Each summer, Uncle Pow took us fishing on the river, and when we were twelve, he helped us build a fort in the woods near the ruins of the haunted shot tower. Technically, we weren't supposed to go near the shot tower, which was dangerously

THE HAUNTED TOWER

decrepit and half sunken into the ground, its door long buried beneath soil and creepers. But Frank and I loved visiting the tower because it was said to be haunted by the spirit of a woman who wept and clawed at the walls, begging for someone to let her out. It gave us shivers every time we looked at the tower. We talked about visiting it at night to see if we could see the ghost.

Before we could try it, Mama found out about our fort and scolded us fiercely for disobeying her and dragging poor, simple Uncle Pow into our illicit schemes. "It's dishonorable to take advantage of an old man who can't remember things because of a head injury," she said. "I'm ashamed of you boys!" As punishment, she gave us extra chores for an entire month.

Frank was flattened by Mama's words. We'd been dishonorable. We'd taken advantage of Uncle Pow's head injury. It was a hard condemnation to bear.

"I'm going to become a brain doctor and fix Uncle Pow's head so he remembers everything he forgot," Frank told me at the end of our twelfth summer. Lighthearted Frank was so serious that I believed him at once.

True to his word, Frank studied hard and got into a famous university. He studied some more and got into medical school. Then he went to Europe to study with a famous brain surgeon and learned everything that science could teach him about the brain.

Almost fifty years to the day after Uncle Pow was brought home to the plantation with the wound that shattered his skull and his wits, Frank came home from his sojourn in Europe and told the family that he could heal Uncle Powhatan.

"It is a very simple surgery," Frank told the gathered family. "Six times out of ten, the person's memory is completely restored."

We were dubious. Uncle Pow was happy as he was. Wouldn't it be kinder to let things be after all this time? All the people he'd known and loved fifty years ago were long gone now. But Frank was adamant. He'd spent his life studying medicine so he could help Uncle Pow. No one would stand between him and his goal. And no one did. Uncle Pow was brought to the hospital, where he beamed proudly at his great-nephew-the-doctor and told the nurses lovely stories about the animals he cared for on the plantation. No one could have been happier going into surgery than Great-Uncle Powhatan.

Frank and I were both beside him when the old man woke after the surgery. He blinked hazily and stared from face to familiar face, a pucker between his eyebrows.

"Where am I?" he snapped briskly after inspecting us for a long moment. "What is this place?"

It was the voice of a stranger. Gone was the happy smile, the languid tone. His voice was deeper, with the authoritative tone of a colonel.

"Where are my men?" Uncle Pow demanded. "Did we win the battle?"

He gasped suddenly and struggled to sit up. "Annabelle! I must rescue Annabelle. She's all alone in the tower!"

Alarmed, we pushed Uncle Pow back onto the bed. Frank said, "It's us, Uncle Powhatan. Frank and Tom. Remember? We are your great-nephews."

"Don't talk nonsense. I have no nephews. My sister is an infant," the old man cried. He thrashed about so fiercely that he knocked both of us to the floor. As the nurse came running with a sedative, Frank and I stared at each other in horror. Uncle Pow didn't remember us. His past had returned in full, but he retained no knowledge of anything that had occurred after his accident!

The old man calmed under the sedative, but not for long. When it wore off, he began thrashing again, crying, "Annabelle! My wife! Annabelle. You must help her!"

Frank and I stared at each other again, this time in consternation. Great-Uncle Powhatan was married? I'd known him all my life, and no one had mentioned a wife.

For three days the old man thrashed and screamed whenever he came out of sedation. No one could calm him, and he recognized none of his family. Uncle Pow grew weaker each time he regained consciousness, and it was soon apparent that the old man was dying in great agony of mind and spirit.

Frank's agony was as great as that of the old man he had spent his whole life trying to help. Hoping his home environment might ease his suffering, Frank brought Uncle Pow to the plantation, where Mama and I shared the burden of caring for the old man in his last days.

Frank and I were with Uncle Pow when he woke on the fourth afternoon after the surgery. As consciousness approached, Uncle Pow's face contorted with pain, and his right hand crept to his head to claw futilely at the bandage. A spasm of remorse crossed Frank's face as he clutched Uncle Pow's hand and begged him to rest. Uncle Pow's eyes shot open when he heard Frank's voice. Taking in his white coat and air of authority, Uncle Powhatan pulled Frank close to him.

"Listen to me, doctor," he gasped. "I am dying, and there isn't much time. I am a colonel in the Confederate army. I was given a few hours' leave between battles to go to church and marry my sweetheart, Annabelle, who lived in the town where our division was camped. We met at the church. Annabelle was wearing a blue silk wedding gown, and I was all slicked up in my best Confederate uniform. After the wedding, we went down to the river with a picnic lunch for a few hours of honeymooning before I was due back at my camp. Suddenly we heard a terrible blast from the woods in front of us. Annabelle thought it was an approaching thunderstorm, but I knew the sound of cannon fire. The Yankees were attacking my base camp."

The old man fell back on the pillows, gasping for breath. Uncle Pow coughed repeatedly, and blood leaked from the corner of his mouth when he spoke again. "I had to get back to my men, but I couldn't abandon my new wife. The battle was almost upon us when I thought of the old shot tower. Acrid smoke stung our nostrils, and bullets winged through the air as we ran across the meadow."

The old man fell silent a moment, eyes fixed on some spot over Frank's shoulder, his face a rictus of remembered terror. "There was a dry cistern in the tower. I lowered Annabelle into it using an old rope. 'I will be back in a few hours, my dearest love, as soon as the soldiers are gone,' I told my Annabelle. Then I covered the cistern with the stone lid, leaving my wife alone in pitch blackness, and ran back into the woods, hoping to rejoin my company and defeat the Yankees before they found my bride's hiding place. I must have been shot as soon as I left the tower, because the next thing I remember is waking up in this hospital."

The old man's eyes focused suddenly on Frank's face. "It's been days since I left Annabelle in that black cistern," he cried. "There was no food or water down there. Please, you must go to her. You must rescue her! Run, boy. Go *now!*"

Uncle Pow's body arched in a sudden seizure, and a moment later he fell dead against the bedclothes. Frank stared at the old man's corpse in horror. Then he ran. He had to. The force of the old man's last words thrust him out the door and down the stairs before conscious thought kicked in. I followed, as compelled by the old man's story as Frank appeared to be. We did not slow when we reached the toolshed, even knowing that whatever had happened to Annabelle had happened long ago. Frank threw hammers and saws and lumber out of his way, frantically searching for a shovel.

"I'm sure someone heard her cries and let her out," I said to Frank as he grimly thrust a pickax at me. Frank grabbed a shovel for himself and raced away without answering, galloping down the river path that led to our childhood fort.

I followed at a run, remembering all the stories I'd heard about the haunted tower. Folks said the ghost became very active during a thunderstorm, screaming and scratching and begging for help. And Uncle Pow had said that Annabelle mistook the cannon fire for an approaching thunderstorm.

Oh, dear God! Was *Uncle Pow's wife* the origin of the ghost story?

Frank reached the dilapidated tower ahead of me. He started shoveling around the half-buried door as I attacked the hardened turf with my pickax. When the sunken door was revealed, Frank kicked his way through the rotted wood and grimly tore away miles of rustling dead vines that hid the stone cover in the floor. It took all our combined strength to lift the cover, and I marveled that a young Uncle Pow had moved it alone.

As we opened the pit, we were overwhelmed by the smell of musty old air and perfumed decay. A ray of golden light from the setting sun pierced through the shattered remains of the tower door and shone into the cistern at our feet. I stared in horror at the huddled heap of bones and blue silk, which was all that remained of my Great-Aunt Annabelle. There were deep vertical gouges in the wall above her skull where she'd tried to claw her way out of the black pit. And a golden wedding band gleamed on the bones of one hand.

Handprints

The kids in my high school had been telling scary stories about Crawford Road all week. It was driving me crazy. It was October, and everyone I knew had caught the paranormal bug. I tried to ignore them. I was busy with college applications and honors courses. I was waiting with bated breath to see if I'd gotten into Virginia Tech, and spooky stories seemed a stupid distraction compared to my future.

I was still grumbling about the supernatural frenzy that had gripped the senior class as my best friend Sharon and I slipped into a booth at the local pizza place after our track meet on Friday night.

"I have heard twenty different Crawford Road stories so far this week," I moaned. "Twenty! We live in Yorktown, for crying out loud. There's a huge battlefield right here! And Williamsburg is right down the road. You would think we'd have ghostly soldier sightings galore. Maybe some phantom cannon fire. But no. Apparently the only haunted place in the *entire region* is Crawford Road!"

Sharon chuckled. "I hate to break it to you, but here comes another fan of Crawford Road."

HANDPRINTS

That was the only warning I got before James slid into the booth beside me and grinned across at his little sister. My face heated up and I wanted to melt through the floor. I'd been crushing on Sharon's older brother for years, and I had yet to utter a coherent sentence in his presence.

James was a year older than us and had recently started his freshman year at Virginia Tech. The new college man boldly proclaimed that he would pay for our dinner, and we were happy to agree. After we ordered, Sharon told James that I'd applied to his school. His whole face lit up when he heard this news.

"We could be neighbors next year," James said with a smile that made my heart beat faster.

I very bravely asked him how he liked school so far and managed to make the question sound almost intelligent. (Progress!) James was eager to talk about his college adventures. He described his classes, his extracurricular activities, and what it was like to live in the dorm with his friends. I hung on his every word, picturing what my life might be like if I went to Virginia Tech next year.

It wasn't until the pizza arrived, overflowing with toppings and smelling divine, that James moved on to ghost stories. He and his college roommate had started watching paranormal shows and had spent the last few weekends checking out haunted places near the school.

"Tommy wanted to come home with me this weekend, but he got pulled into an important lab project, so I'm here on my own."

"Wh . . . where are you investigating this weekend?" I stuttered, still a bit overwhelmed by his nearness.

"I'am going to see if I could get some EMF readings down by the bridge at Crawford Road. Would you ladies like to join me?" James asked.

Overwhelmed as I was by sharing a booth with him, I'd forgotten Sharon's earlier reference to James and his obsession with Crawford Road. Now I stared at him in shock. *Et tu,* James?

Fortunately for my heart, Sharon knew the correct answer. Before I stuck my foot in my mouth, Sharon accepted for us both and swept me out to James's car while he settled the pizza bill.

"Think of it as an almost date," Sharon hissed, shoving me into the front seat. "It's good practice for next year."

For some strange reason, Sharon had always been convinced that I was going to marry her brother. I never knew why, since I consistently failed to string two sentences together when he was present.

James slid into the driver's seat and gestured to the backseat. "Equipment's in the bag. Let's go find a ghost!"

"Jilly is a paranormal skeptic," Sharon told her brother from the backseat. "You will have to convert her."

"Really?" James said, glancing over at me for a split second before turning his attention to the dark road ahead. "You don't believe in ghosts?"

"I prefer science," I said. "If I can see it or hear it or touch it, I can believe in it."

James nodded. "I appreciate that. It's why I bring all the electronic gear along. It helps me prove that the paranormal is real. If I can capture the sounds, if I can see it with my eyes, feel a chill where none should exist, it helps prove to me that something is out there. In a way, tonight is a paranormal research experiment."

I nodded despite myself. That sounded interesting. "I will try to keep an open mind," I told him.

I realized suddenly that I wasn't stuttering. Sharon always said James would like the real me if I could just get over my shyness enough to let him get to know me. He'd taken the "paranormal skeptic" news in stride, so maybe Sharon was right. As things stood right now, I had nothing to lose.

So, I started describing all the stories the seniors were telling one another about Crawford Road and how it drove me crazy that they were so focused on an urban legend when we had all this American history surrounding us. I was astonished by my eloquence, given my present company. James listened attentively and asked good questions that showed he was following my logic.

"That's a great point," James said when I finally paused for breath. "Maybe we can do some historical ghost hunting on Sunday night before I head back to school."

I blinked several times in surprise and said, "Sure. I'd like that."

"Okay, ladies. Here we go," James said, flipping on his blinker and turning into a narrow, tree-lined road. "Keep your eyes and ears open. Between the murders that have taken place along this road, the car accidents, and the bridge where the bride supposedly hanged herself, there are multiple opportunities to experience the paranormal."

The short residential portion of the road seemed average enough. But when we entered the wooded portion that wound through the park, I felt a lump in my stomach. The headlights lit various parts of the scene around me: a crooked tree with twisted branches like clutching fingers, a bush with shaking leaves but no wind, a fallen trunk that for one heart-stopping moment resembled a dead body. I had to get my imagination under control or I'd run screaming from the car long before we reached the bridge.

In the backseat, Sharon was experimenting with some of James's contraptions.

"Can we get EMF readings in a moving car?" she asked as James negotiated a curve.

"Probably not anything I'd trust," James told her. "Wait until we get out at the bridge."

I was not eager to stop. While I didn't believe in the paranormal, I did believe in the murders that had taken place on this road. Putting oneself in a remote location late at night seemed like a bad idea.

Worse, a fog seemed to be creeping down upon us. Wisps were appearing along the edges of the woods and rising slowly to obscure the view in front and behind. James slowed the car, cussing softly under his breath.

"I'm not sure if this is a good sign or a terrible one," he said softly to me, while Sharon continued to poke around with the EMF detector in the backseat. "We should be nearing the bri . . ."

His words cut off abruptly when the car thudded and shook, as if we'd run over something. I gave a shriek of surprise, and James hit the brakes.

"There wasn't anything in front of us!" I cried. "What did we hit? Where did it come from?"

"I don't know," James shouted, leaping out of the driver's seat. Sharon and I were close on his heels.

We searched all around the car. Nothing was there. The foggy headlights did little to illuminate the gloom, so we grabbed flashlights from James's paranormal equipment bags and searched under the car and then all along the verge on both sides. Still nothing.

"There's not even a pothole," I exclaimed as we clustered beside the car, our faces pale and strained in the glow of the headlights. "Nothing to explain what caused that thump."

"Ghosts," whispered Sharon.

I was in no mood to scoff. I pointed to the backseat of the car. "Maybe you should see if you can get an EMF reading."

James pulled out the device and scanned in the vicinity of the car while Sharon and I kept a lookout for approaching vehicles.

"The readings are higher than normal," James said. "But I can't tell if there are any power lines here that might be affecting it. It's too foggy and dark. Come on. It's not safe to linger here in the middle of the road. Let's keep going."

James started the car and drove slowly through the mist. I glanced out the side window and felt my skin crawl. The window was slowly fogging up, revealing two glowing handprints on the glass. There was something menacing in the position of the fingers, as if they were poised to lock around my neck.

"James . . ." I gasped. "James, stop right now."

James hit the brakes. "What's wrong?" he asked, turning to me. Then he saw the handprints.

"Oh my lord," Sharon gasped from the backseat.

Cold shivers were running up and down my body. I shrank away from the window, leaning toward James, who was hyperventilating with shock.

"Make it stop," I whispered.

Just then, something banged sharply on the roof, shaking the car. Wham. Wham. Wham!

Each blow reverberated through the car as the roof flexed inward and then rebounded back to its normal shape. The handprints on the passenger window glowed brighter. I cringed into the bottom of my seat.

"Get us out of here," Sharon shouted from the back.

James threw the car into gear as something slammed heavily against the trunk. We screamed, and James hit the gas. The car fishtailed wildly for a moment until the wheels caught a dry spot on the pavement. Then we raced madly down the foggy lane.

The dark shape of the bridge loomed up suddenly in the headlights. Directly in front of us I saw a glowing translucent mass rocking back and forth dementedly, halfway between the roof of the bridge and the ground below. It looked like a hanged body.

In the backseat, Sharon screamed in panic. My throat was so tight I couldn't even gasp. Oh my lord, why had I agreed to come on this insane ride?

"I'm going in," James gritted through his teeth. "No choice."

The car drove straight through the center of the swirling mass, but there was no thud or impact. Just a bone-chilling sense of something . . . other . . . passing through my body. It was the mother of all cold spots, and it was in that moment that I became a true believer in the paranormal.

We were past the bridge in a second. I heard Sharon throwing up in the backseat. James's face was several shades paler in the dim light of the car. He was gripping the wheel so tightly his knuckles were white, and driving as fast as he safely could on the narrow, windy road.

"I . . . I think that was sufficient evidence for me," I gasped finally, trying to break the terrified silence. I glanced out the side window and saw that the handprints were fading away.

"We didn't even need the equipment," Sharon agreed from behind me, wiping her mouth on her sleeve. "I'm sorry about the seat, James. I'll clean it up."

"N . . . no worries," her brother said shakily. "I'd have done the same thing if I wasn't driving. Let's go home."

I was accepted into Virginia Tech on Wednesday the following week. And on Halloween night, James took me out on our first date. We went to a haunted corn maze. It was pretty tame stuff after our adventure on Crawford Road, which was just fine with me.

PART TWO
Powers of Darkness and Light

19

River Witch

It was bad luck to go fishing on a Sunday. Everyone in town knew that. Everyone except Jonah.

Jonah was a big strong man who worked as a carpenter in Farmville. Most everyone in town liked him, but they all knew that his weakness was fishing. Jonah would go fishing every chance he got, even on Sundays when everyone else was in church. And that got folks in town riled up. There was a rumor—started so long ago no one could remember the details—that bad luck would come to anyone who fished that part of the river on a Sunday. For decades, pious folks had avoided the river on the Lord's Day, just to be safe.

Jonah laughed when he heard the bad luck rumors. He figured folks were trying to scare him into going to church, so he took delight in proving them wrong. When the deacons told Jonah he wouldn't catch any fish on the Sabbath, he carried a stringer full of trout into the churchyard after the morning service and presented them to the preacher. When the Sunday school teachers told Jonah that any fish he caught on the Lord's Day would choke him and kill him, he roasted his catch on a fire in his front yard and ate them where everyone could see.

RIVER WITCH

Jonah was incorrigible, and the despair of his neighbors. If he hadn't been such a good carpenter, folks would have run him out of town.

Now old Granny Clarkson, who was pushing one hundred years, shook her head whenever someone spoke about Jonah and his fishing problem. She remembered the source of the bad luck rumors, and Jonah's defiance troubled her.

"My parents warned us to stay away from the river," she said to her daughter-in-law, knitting needles clicking as she rocked in her porch chair. "There's a River Witch that rules those waters, and she's always looking for new subjects. She can't touch pious folks who honor the Sabbath. But someone like Jonah who dishonors the Lord's Day could easily fall under her spell. I've seen it happen before to a distant cousin of mine who wouldn't listen to our warnings."

"There's no such thing as a River Witch, Granny," her daughter-in-law said with an indulgent smile.

Granny Clarkson sighed and reminded herself that Lally grew up in the Blue Ridge Mountains and didn't have much experience with the waters around Farmville.

Now, the young 'uns in town were all on Jonah's side. They thought the old folks were too strict and there was no such thing as bad luck. The more Jonah stuck to his ways, the more the young 'uns admired him. Some of them started skipping Sunday school to go fishing. Even the Clarkson grandsons tried it once, but Granny laid down the law so emphatically that they were the first ones in the sanctuary the next Sunday.

While the erring Clarkson grandsons sat praying in their pew, Jonah sat on the riverbank fishing for hours in his favorite spot. He was having no luck at all. He was just about to pack up his pole and go somewhere else when a fish finally bit his hook. It was a mighty big one. Jonah fought and fought with that fish until finally he managed to pull it out of the river. He saw at once that it wasn't a fish at all. It was a strange creature, such as Jonah had never seen before. It had a tail like a fish, but its head was like a duck, and it had wings like an eagle. Frightened, Jonah dropped everything—hook, line, and fishing pole—and ran for home. But the creature started singing:

Come back and pick me up, Jonah,
Come back and pick me up, Jonah,
Domie ninky head, Jonah.

The nonsense words at the end of the song put a spell on Jonah. He came back and picked up his strange "fish." It sang:

Take me to the house, Jonah,
Take me to the house, Jonah,
Domie ninky head, Jonah.

Jonah took the "fish" up to the house. He was in a sort of trance and didn't notice when some of the youngsters who had skipped church that day followed him down the street, murmuring in wonder at the strange fish he had caught on the Lord's Day. The creature sang:

Clean me up and cook me, Jonah,
Clean me up and cook me, Jonah,
Domie ninky head, Jonah.

So Jonah cleaned the creature and cooked it up. He hoped that once it was dead, it would stop singing to him. But no sooner had Jonah's "fish" finished cooking when it sang:

Take me off and eat me, Jonah,
Take me off and eat me, Jonah,

Domie ninky head, Jonah.

By this time the church service was over. Everyone bustled out of the sanctuary and went searching for the source of the commotion. Old Granny Clarkson took one look and herded her family home, her wrinkled face grim. She'd seen this once before.

There was great consternation when the townspeople heard Jonah's fish singing to him. The old folks said it was the wrath of God come upon Jonah for fishing on Sunday. The young 'uns just laughed.

Still caught up in the spell, Jonah took his "fish" off the fire and began to eat it. He was too scared to eat more than a bite or two, but his dinner kept singing:

Eat me up, Jonah,
Eat me up, Jonah,
Domie ninky head, Jonah.

So Jonah ate the whole thing, even though he thought the "fish" would choke him. As soon as he finished the last bite, Jonah started to swell up. He got bigger and bigger and bigger until he burst in a shower of flesh, blood, and bone. The River Witch stepped out of his shattered body, whole and alive.

The townsfolk gasped and drew back in fear as the creature walked past them all, down to the river. It was singing again:

Don't you fish on Sunday, Jonah,
Don't you fish on Sunday, Jonah,
Domie ninky head, Jonah.

When it reached the mossy bank, the River Witch slid back under the water, and no one ever saw it again.

The next Sunday, every adult in Farmville was sitting in the church sanctuary a quarter of an hour before the start of service, and all the young 'uns were back in Sunday school. Because it was bad luck to go fishing on a Sunday. Everyone in town knew that. Now.

20

The Witch's Shoulder

BIG LAUREL, WISE COUNTY

One day, out of the clear blue, my sheep started dropping dead in the field. I'm a shepherd, so I've seen sheep pass in my time. But these sheep were bursting with health afore they up and died. One minute they'd be butting heads or gamboling playfully; the next moment they were flat on the ground—dead as a doornail.

"I just don't understand it," I said to my wife the night a fifth sheep keeled over in the middle of the field. "There ain't nothing wrong with them. I had the sheep doc in to check the lot of them. He even opened up one of the dead ones to have a look. They are fine. So why are they dropping like flies?"

My wife shook her head. "If you ask me, I'd say they were bewitched. Maybe you'd better talk to the conjure woman that lives over on the plantation and see what she says."

I hadn't thought of asking the conjure woman. But the doc hadn't helped at all, *and* he'd charged me a big fee to boot. I didn't have anything to lose by consulting the conjure woman, so I hied over to the plantation come sundown and asked around until I found the conjure lady cooking over the fire in a cabin packed with young 'uns. As soon as she saw me, she sent

THE WITCH'S SHOULDER

them young 'uns up to the loft to play and sat me down with a cup of tea.

"What's the problem?" she asked. She had a sweet, sympathetic face, and my troubles just poured out of me at the sight of her compassionate dark eyes. I told her about my sheep dying and the doc charging me to do nothing and my fear that I'd lose the whole flock. She listened intently and then asked me to describe each death in detail. When I finished, she gave a deep sigh and sat back in her chair.

"Honey, you done got you a bad curse on that flock of yours."

"That's what my wife said," I agreed with a sigh.

"I'm gonna tell you how to break this curse. And you best follow my instructions to the letter, or more of your sheep are gonna die."

When I solemnly promised to follow her instructions to the letter, she told me what to do. And she made me repeat it back to her to be sure I got it right. Then she gave me some biscuits to take home to my wife and shooed me out of the cabin afore her young 'uns—who were making a hullabaloo—came crashing down through the ceiling.

My wife came a-running out the front door when she saw me coming up the lane with my lantern.

"What did the conjure woman say?" she gasped.

"You were right. Them sheep are cursed," I said and told her everything the conjure woman had told me.

I got up early the next morning, determined to follow the conjure woman's instructions to the letter. I went to the barn where I'd placed the fifth dead sheep and carefully carved out the shoulder. Then I went into the kitchen, where my wife had reduced the fire in the stove to a bunch of warm coals. Very carefully we put the shoulder in the oven to bake. The conjure woman had told us to warm it up real slow before baking it for the best results. And she told us that if anyone came to our house, we weren't to let them borrow or steal anything from the house, and on no account were we to give them anything to eat or drink. It sounded a bit strange, but I'd promised to obey her instructions, and that's what I was gonna do.

It took two hours for that sheep shoulder to warm up to the point where it was ready for baking. Nobody had stopped by up to that point, and I'd just about decided nobody was gonna when my wife hurried to the window, crying "Look!"

Our neighbor's wife was hurrying up the lane toward us, though it was too early for a sociable call. She knocked on the door, and we let her in, watching her closely. She wanted to borrow some meal, but we told her we were out of meal. Then she asked for a drink of water, but my quick-witted wife told her that we'd drunk the last of the water from the well and had to go back for more. Then she hustled the neighbor-woman out the door so fast she didn't have time to steal anything from the house.

Our behavior must have seemed strange, but we weren't taking any chances. The conjure lady had said that anyone might be the witch.

A quarter hour later, the fellow who assisted me in the sheep field arrived. I sent him off with the flock without letting him inside the house. I hoped he wasn't the witch, but appearances could be deceiving, as the conjure lady had been quick to tell me. Even the minister came by to drop off some pamphlets for my wife to distribute at the Ladies Aid meeting, which she was having at our house the next day but one.

"Surely the minister isn't a witch," my wife exclaimed when she saw him riding his horse up the lane. But I made her go outside to greet him, and she took the pamphlets before he could dismount from his horse. All the while, inside the house the smell of roasting sheep shoulder was gradually filling the downstairs.

As my wife waved the minister off down the lane, the neighbor-woman came hurrying up, looking even more agitated than before. She met my wife in the yard and begged her for some salt.

"I'm afraid we ain't got no salt," I said from the doorway.

"No salt! Surely you do. Let me look," said the neighbor-woman, and she barged right past me into the house. My wife and I followed her quickly, exchanging alarmed glances.

"No salt," my wife said firmly, blocking the pantry door with her body.

The neighbor-woman twitched and turned to glare at our oven, where the shoulder was slowly getting hot. "I'm thirsty," she said fretfully. "Did you get the water from the well yet?"

"We've been a tad busy this morning," I said, firmly shoving her toward the door. "I ain't had time."

The neighbor-woman slipped past me again and tried to knock open the oven door.

"What are you roasting in there?" she asked. I blocked the oven door with my shepherd's crook before she could get it open.

"So nice of you to call," my wife said then, stepping in front of the neighbor-woman and taking her firmly by the arm. (Was it me, or did the neighbor woman wince when my wife jostled her shoulder?) A moment later the neighbor-woman was walking down the lane, with frequent looks back over her shoulder.

"Could it be her?" I asked my wife as soon as our neighbor disappeared from view. "She's acting awful strange."

"I bet it is her," my wife replied. "Remember last month when her husband wanted to buy our property with the stream running through it to pasture his cows? And you said no because we needed it for our sheep. I bet this is his wife's revenge against us for refusing to sell."

"You could be right," I said thoughtfully. The husband hadn't seemed too bothered by my refusal, but his wife had taken it as a personal insult.

My wife added a few more sticks to the fire as we spoke, and the sheep shoulder started to sizzle inside the oven. It was turning a nice brown color when we heard running footsteps coming down the lane. Afore I reached the front door, the neighbor-woman burst inside. "For God's sake, get the shoulder off the fire! Get it off quick! You're killing me!" She tore off the sleeve covering her left shoulder with shaking fingers. Underneath her dress, the woman's shoulder was the same deep shade of brown as the roasting shoulder of mutton, and I could hear it sizzling.

"Are you done cursing my sheep?" I asked sternly.

"I'm done! I'm done. Take it off the fire," she begged.

"Swear to it," my wife said, equally stern, and made her repeat the magic words the conjure lady had taught us. They were just gibberish to us, but they meant something to the neighbor-woman. She turned real pale, and I could tell she didn't want to say them. But her shoulder was burning up before our eyes, and she had no choice. When she uttered the last word, a mighty thunderclap came right out of a clear-blue sky; the neighbor-woman fell to her knees sobbing.

That's that, I thought, and I took the mutton off the fire. The neighbor-woman gasped with relief, and my wife gave her a wet cloth and some soothing ointment to put on her burned shoulder before sternly sending her away.

"Should we tell her husband she's a witch?" I asked my wife when the woman was gone.

"No need," my wife replied. "If he doesn't already know, he'll figure it out when he sees her shoulder. Besides," she added thoughtfully, "I think them magic words the conjure woman gave us may have taken her witchcraft away from her. They were that strong!"

Remembering the thunderclap, I had to agree.

That evening I went to the conjure lady's house with a big basket of vegetables and fruit from my garden and a lamb from my flock. I told her the whole story, and a grin spread all over her beautiful round face.

"Honey, she won't never bother you again," the conjure lady promised.

And she never did.

21

The Fiddler and the Wolves

The whole family was invited to a house-raising in Grayson County, and everyone was plumb excited about the occasion. Not that it weren't hard work, but it was also a chance to meet up with folks from all around the county. When the work's done, everyone gathers in the field for a big dance and a feast. All the ladies bake and fry and roast for days beforehand, getting ready for that feast and trying to outdo one another with their fancy recipes.

Now music is an essential part of any dance, so one of the slaves on our plantation, Ned by name, was specially invited to the house-raising on account of Ned could fiddle like no one's business. He was in demand all around the county whenever anyone threw a party. Ned agreed to come, but he had a mess of work that needed doing on the farm, so he told the family he'd start out after the work was done.

"Just be sure you arrive in plenty of time for the dance," the Missus told Ned.

"And be careful of the wolves," the Master added. "I hear there are several packs roaming around the hills, and they are very aggressive."

THE FIDDLER AND THE WOLVES

Ned promised to arrive in time for the dance and to watch out for wolves. Then he went to finish mending the fence in the cow pasture while the family headed to the house-raising. Once the fence was mended, Ned had to track down all the cows that had strayed from the pasture, which took more time than he expected. He started off late for the house-raising and had to run whenever there was a flat bit in order to make up some time. Not an easy task in these mountains, but Ned was young and fleet of foot.

Ned had to slow down on the steep bits, and dusk found him picking his way carefully up the trail at the top of the mountain with his violin clutched under one arm. Suddenly he heard a wolf howl in the woods to his left. The hairs on the back of his neck pricked at the sound, and he heard two answering howls from the woods to his right. He stepped up the pace, his skin breaking out in a cold sweat. It would not take the pack long to gather once they got his scent.

Ned started to run, his heart thumping so hard his ribs hurt. There were more howls now, coming closer together and closing the gap with him. What should he do? What should he do? His brain was frozen with panic, but his feet kept running. He tripped again and again over roots and large stones, but he kept going. Once his foot slipped on some loose gravel and he almost went down. Going down would be his death, he knew. His fiddle slipped in his grasp, and he clutched at it frantically as he fought to regain his balance. With a jolt that shot pain through his bones, his left foot found firm ground and he was running again down the steep path as a wolf howled in the woods beside him.

His chest felt searing hot, his lungs strained so hard he thought they would burst, and a huge stitch bent him sideways in agony. But he kept running. There were still several miles to go before he reached the new homestead. He'd never make it. He could hear wolves running through the bracken on either side of the path, and a couple of wolves howled right behind him.

Ned clutched his fiddle, put on speed he didn't know he had, and swerved to the right at the fork in the trail instead of taking the turnoff for the new homestead. He vaguely remembered a tumbled-down old cabin about halfway down the mountain. It was his only hope now. The wolves were snarling behind him, and the gap between them was closing . . . closing . . .

He spotted the cabin up ahead, and it gave him strength. He made his legs go faster. Faster. Then his heart leapt in dismay. There was a huge pile of debris in front of the door, and the wolves were nearly upon him. He threw himself at the portal and wrenched it open, debris flying everywhere. He was inside in a flash and slammed the door on the paws of the leading wolf. It howled in agony and fell away among its comrades, who slammed themselves against the door in frustration, snarling and howling at Ned, who pushed back against it with all his might.

He dropped the fiddle on the floor and reached with a free hand to grab the bar that was propped beside the door. It would buy him a little time. As soon as he was barricaded inside, he grabbed the violin and clambered up onto the joists below the roof. The door would not hold for long, and he fervently prayed that he was high enough to keep him safe from the wolves.

It took ten minutes for the wolves to knock down the door to the cabin. Once inside, they yelped and snarled in frustration when they saw their prey just out of reach. Wolf after wolf jumped up, trying to reach the trembling Ned. He clutched his violin to his chest and kicked at the wolves as they jumped, trying to keep them off balance. He was just beyond their reach until one enterprising wolf leapt onto the back of another and managed to rip a piece from Ned's pant leg. It nearly knocked Ned off his perch into the midst of the writhing pack below him.

Ned gasped and drew up his legs. This infuriated the pack, and their leaps became more spectacular as they used one another as springboards in their efforts to reach their prey.

Ned suddenly had an idea. Balancing precariously, he pulled out the fiddle and scraped his bow jarringly across the strings. The sound hurt the wolves' ears and made them howl and shy away from him. Ned made the violin sing as high as it could go. Several wolves howled and ran out the door. The rest of the pack shivered and cowered back—but not for long. Gradually they became accustomed to the noise and recommenced their attack.

Suddenly one of the wolves leapt so high it got a paw on the plank beside Ned. It overbalanced and fell, but Ned knew this was serious. One of them would make it up here soon, and then he was dead. He put aside the fiddle and drew his knife. He'd heard that wolves would attack anything that was bleeding. Time to find out if it was true.

Ned's sweaty fingers shook against the handle of the knife as he crouched low over the planks. Strange that his hands were sweating, he thought, when he felt so cold inside. He slashed at the next wolf that reached the planks, nearly cutting off its ear. The wolf fell back among its brethren, who snarled and ripped the wolf to shreds before Ned's horrified eyes. He knew the same thing would happen to him if he fell.

Fortunately, in the melee that followed, a second wolf was injured; the pack fell upon it as well. It was at that moment that the darkness outside was illuminated by the light of many torches and Ned heard men's voices calling his name.

"Here! I'm in here," he screamed out over the barks and growls of the wolves.

The men outside gave a loud shout when they heard his voice, and the wolves panicked, scrambling this way and that in their effort to escape. Ned heard musket shots as the pack streamed outside the cabin, and in a moment the wolves were gone.

With a mighty gasp of relief, Ned fell back against the planks, and that's where his master found him a moment later.

"Dear God, that was close," the Master said, helping the shaking lad down from the joists. "We got worried when you didn't show up and came hunting for you."

"I was a goner until you showed up," Ned told him thankfully.

"You even saved the fiddle," marveled one of the other men. Ned gave a weak grin. "The wolves didn't like the fiddle music much," he said.

"They may not, but we do," said the owner of the new homestead. "Come on, son. You could do with some feasting, and we could do with some fiddling."

The men escorted Ned back along the path and down the road toward the feast. Up on the hillside, a lone wolf howled in vain.

22

The White Dove

DANVILLE

Our mistress was the prettiest lady in the country. Everyone thought so. She and the Master were so much in love that they billed and cooed all day long like a pair of doves. It made us smile to watch them.

The Mistress loved to putter in the flower garden, and we liked to watch her watering her rose bushes or doing her embroidery near the fragrant snowball bush. Sometimes the young master would sneak up behind her and cover her eyes with his hands. She'd laugh and pretend she didn't know who he was. We laughed right along with her, and everyone would smile when he swept her up into his arms for a kiss.

Everyone on the plantation loved the young mistress. She knew everyone who worked there by name, and if any one of us took sick, she'd tend to us herself with her basket of herbal remedies. She was a good woman.

Sometimes when the day's work was through, me and my family would sit outside our little cabin watching the moon rise over the trees and counting the stars. That's what we were doing the night of the party on midsummer's eve. The big house was all alight with lanterns and candles in every window.

THE WHITE DOVE

We sat watching the moon and listening to the folks laughing and talking up the hill. One of my boys was good with a fiddle, and after a while we heard him playing his heart out for the guests. The music sure sounded pretty in the moonlight.

And then a terrible screech cut across the music. We saw a whitish bird flit across the moon and land on the roof of the big house. It was an owl. My mama, who was dozing in her favorite chair, woke with a start as the owl screeched again.

"Lordy," she said, tying a knot into her apron string. "Where's that bird at, Lizzie?"

"He landed on the roof of the big house," I said, pointing him out. That screech owl was clear as day, sitting on the gable over the master and mistress's bedroom.

"That's not good. Not good a-tall," Mama said, turning the pockets of her apron inside out as the owl screeched again. I stared at Mama, round eyed. She always said that screech owls brought bad luck to a house, but she didn't like to talk about it much except to warn us to turn our apron or pants pockets inside out if we heard one.

"Why ain't it good, Mama?" my husband, John, asked, laying a comforting hand on my neck when I shivered.

The owl shrieked again, a lonely sound against the laughter and music coming from the big house.

"It means someone in the big house is gonna die," Mama said, tying a third knot in her apron string.

Someone is gonna die, I thought, shivering and moving closer to my man. Overhead, the owl shrieked again, his lonely cry echoing forebodingly in my mind long after he flew away.

A week later, the young master and mistress were walking in the flower garden at dusk when the young mistress fainted.

She had spotted a new kind of flower growing near the snowball bush and was reaching down to examine it when dizziness overcame her. I was retrieving the wash from the clothesline when it happened and ran to help. The Master sent me for the doctor, and I scampered off right quick. I remembered the screech owl that had come to the big house on the night of the party, and I was scared. I loved the young mistress; I didn't want her to die.

The young mistress lay in her bed for a week with a high fever and didn't recognize anyone who came into the room, not even the Master. The Master asked me to come tend to the young mistress while she was ill. I did my best to follow the doctor's instructions, and when the young master was out of the room, I slipped her some of the herbal remedies Mama mixed up at our cabin. Nothing helped.

I was in the room the day the young mistress died. The good Lord helped her recover her senses long enough to say good-bye to the folks that loved her, which was a mercy. She thanked the doctor for tending her, and she touched my cheek and told me how grateful she was to me for everything I'd done for her since she first came to the big house as a bride. Then she took hold of the young master's hand and told him that she loved him with her whole heart. She said she would send a white dove back to comfort him after she went to heaven. It would perch on the snowball bush she loved so much, and when he heard it cooing, he would know she was there with him.

The young mistress died a few minutes later, still holding his hand.

We were all grieved by the death of the young mistress, but the Master felt it worst. After the funeral, he closed up the big house and went far away to Europe. We weren't sure if he'd ever come back. The seasons passed one by one. I carefully tended the flower garden the young mistress had loved so much, and I watched the snowball bush for a white dove. But the snowball bush drooped and barely bloomed at all. And the white dove never came—neither did the Master.

It must have been two, three years later that we received word that the Master was coming home. And he was bringing a new bride with him. He'd met the daughter of a lord abroad and had married her after an extremely short courtship. The young mistress was forgotten.

We rushed about, cleaning the big house from top to bottom. I took special pains with the flower garden, and that's when I noticed that the snowball bush had bloomed early. And there were more flowers on that bush than I'd ever seen before. It was as if the bush knew the Master was coming home.

We dressed in our finest the day the Master was due home. I was curious to see the new bride who was the daughter of a lord. Would she be a kind and lovely mistress like the Master's first wife?

As soon as I set eyes on the new mistress, my heart sank right down to my toes. Her face was beautiful but proud. Her mouth was pinched, and her dark eyes were narrow and cruel, though she smiled gracefully as we welcomed her. After making a short speech, the Master turned to help his lady into the house. At that moment, a white dove swept down from the sky, nearly brushing the Master's head with its wings. It landed on the snowball bush in the garden, where it lifted its voice in a sad moan.

The Master stood very still, staring at the white dove as all the color drained from his face. His new wife glanced from the dove to her husband, not sure what to make of the situation. After a moment of shocked silence, the Master turned his back on the white dove, offered his arm to his new wife, and escorted her into the house. In the garden, the white dove moaned.

The folks that served dinner that night told Mama and me that the Master barely ate a bite of his food. He kept staring out the window toward the garden and listening to the moans of the white dove. The new mistress was annoyed by his distraction. She spoke sharply to the serving folks, criticized the food, and sent several dishes back to the kitchen. The house servants didn't like her a-tall, and neither did we.

John and I sat outside our door, listening to the white dove and holding hands.

"Do ya think it's the young mistress?" I whispered to him.

"I do," he said. "She done come back like she promised. But she ain't gonna bill and coo like she thought she would, 'cause he married again."

"On account of who he married," Mama called from inside the house.

I thought they both were right.

Things did not go well at the plantation after the Master returned. Oh, the crops did fine, but the new mistress was a piece of work. She used a switch on the housemaids and other folks when they didn't move as promptly as she liked. I stayed out of her way as much as I could. If she ever used that switch on me, I'd take it from her hand and use it right back. Then the Master would sell me away from my family and I'd never see them again. So I steered clear of the new mistress and quietly mourned my young mistress all over again.

I wasn't the only one mourning. Every night at dusk, the white dove would fly down to the snowball bush and moan as if it was dying. It drove the Master crazy and made the new mistress so furious she'd shriek at the serving maids and run crying from the dining room. What made it worse was the way news about the white dove got around to all the neighboring plantations. People came by at dusk to stare over the wall into the garden, and neighbors would make up excuses to visit so they could see the fabled bird.

The Master and his new wife started fighting about the white dove. We could hear them shouting all the way down at the cabin. The new mistress wanted him to kill the dove, but the Master refused. Then the new mistress accused him of not loving her, of marrying her for her money, and the Master would deny it. It was terrible to hear.

At the end of one long argument, the new mistress threatened to return to her family in Europe if the Master didn't do something about the white dove. She meant it too. When she ordered the housemaids to start packing her bags, the Master knew he had lost the battle.

From the front door of our cabin, John and I saw the Master marched down the stairs and out to the garden. When the white dove saw him coming, she fluttered up into the air, cooing tenderly. She flew straight toward the Master, who stopped in his tracks, his mouth twisted with pain. For an instant he watched the white dove approaching him like a woman running to her beloved. Then he pulled out his pistol and shot the white dove in the breast.

A woman's scream echoed and reechoed around the garden, and the white dove fell to the ground, her breast stained red with blood. I clung to John, sobbing as the scream slowly died away. I couldn't bear the look on the Master's face as he turned back to the house where his cruel new bride waited.

We woke the next morning to another woman's scream. It was the new mistress, screaming in terror when she found her husband lying dead at her side. On his face was a smile, and his hands were clenched around a spray of flowers from the snowball bush. When the men lifted his body out of the bed, they found his pillow scattered with the white feathers of a dove.

The new mistress went back to Europe, and her younger, kinder brother took over the plantation. He built a new house several miles from the old one, which was left to rot.

One day I walked over to the old house at dusk to pick a few flowers from the snowball bush and remember the young mistress. The abandoned house looked so sad with its broken windows and sagging roof that it brought tears to my eyes. Finally I turned away and headed down the lane that led home.

Just before a curve in the road obscured the house from sight, I glanced back for a last glimpse of the old homestead. And—in a final blaze from the crimson sky—I saw two white doves fly out of the Master's bedroom window, cooing softly to each other as the sun set.

23

The Black Dog

In the end, he didn't come back. All the rumors, all the malicious gossip, all the sad looks boiled down to one cruel fact: My husband—gone to scout out a new home for us in America— never came back for me. Month after hard month passed with nary a letter, not even a brief note or message sent along with a sea captain. No word. A year passed, then two. And then Civil War came to the Americas, and I lost all hope of hearing from my husband.

I bore it with a brave face as my friends stopped talking about his imminent arrival and my enemies gossiped about another woman or foreign riches, or both. As for my family, they were indignant on my behalf and didn't know what to say. Neither did I. At first I was bewildered and upset. Why hadn't I heard from him? What was causing his long delay? Then I was angry, almost believing the spiteful gossip about another woman. But as the slow years passed, so did my anger. Remembering the love we'd shared, I knew in my heart that James would never leave me for another woman. Something must have happened to him. That was the only explanation.

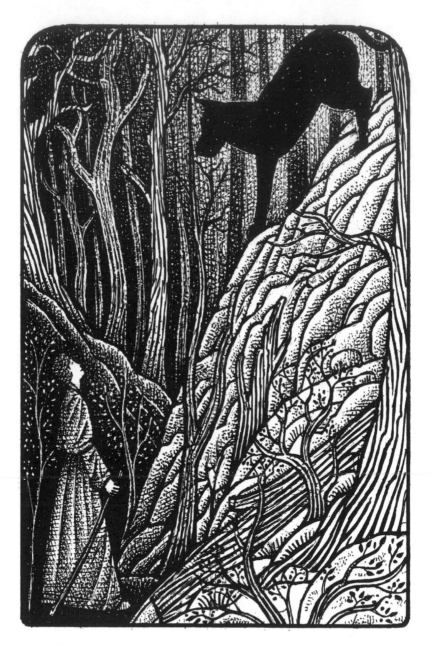

THE BLACK DOG

With this certainty came fear. Was he ill? Dying? I couldn't bring myself to think that he might be dead. My heart rebelled against it. If he was, somehow he'd let me know. My James would never leave me in suspense. He'd cross the divide somehow to speak to me.

My family and friends thought I was being extremely foolish when, on the eighth anniversary of James's departure, I announced that I was traveling to America to look for my husband. The Civil War was ended at last, and I was determined to find him.

"You'll only be hurt again," my mother said.

But I had to know what had happened to him. Even if it turned out he'd left me for another, I had to know. So I booked passage on a ship to Virginia and spent the next several seasick weeks on the high seas. I came ashore at last with only one trunk, a pocket full of money, and an empty head. Somehow I had to find James. Dead or alive, with another woman or waiting faithfully for me, I had to find him.

I was met on the dock by family friends who lived in the area. They welcomed me with open arms and offered me the first comfort I'd had in eight long years. James had stayed with them when he first arrived on his scouting trip to America, and they did not believe for a minute that he had left me. Like me, they were convinced something had happened to him and had done what they could to help me with my search.

We reminisced about old times over dinner, and my friend Alicia said, "The thing I remember best about James's last visit was that huge black hound of his. It was as large as a pony and as gentle as a lamb!"

"Lord, yes!" her husband laughed. "The beast came right into the dining room one night when we were eating roast and begged so solemnly for a taste of beef that we ended up feeding him right from the table. He sat up on his hind legs as if he were a tiny lapdog, and I swear his head was higher than mine was!"

"That sounds just like Solomon," I said with a smile. I missed our dog almost as much as I missed James. "Whenever Solomon wanted something, he reared up on his hind legs, put his paws on James's shoulders, and gazed soulfully into his eyes. Solomon was so big that he could look James right in the eyes— and James was six feet tall!"

I laughed. "He tried it with me once and knocked me right over. He was so upset that he flopped down on the floor beside me and groveled like a puppy! After that, he'd lay his head in my lap and moan when he wanted something from me!"

It felt good to laugh after all the years of pain and worry. Then my friends told me the areas where James had intended to scout for land, and together we planned my journey across Virginia.

It was a long, hard task I'd assigned myself. I stopped at one town after another, inquiring after James and his big black dog. Even after eight years, folks remembered them well. James was a gregarious soul who made a positive impression on everyone he met, and *nobody* could forget Solomon! Much heartened by the news, I followed in James's footsteps, viewing properties he'd prospected, talking to their owners, and staying at the same inns.

At first there was plenty of news about my missing husband. But as I got farther inland, the clues petered out. After six months of searching, I found myself grasping the smallest rumors as if they were precious pearls and trying to keep my heart from despair. Would I never learn the truth about James?

By pure chance, I happened upon a backwoods Virginian who remembered meeting James and Solomon a few years back. It was the first lead I'd had in weeks, and my heart raced with joy as he accurately described my husband and his big black dog. They had last been heard of in Bedford County, where they planned to look at a small plantation for sale. He gave me the approximate location of the plantation and the name of a good inn nearby. My heart raced as I bade him farewell. I felt as if I were getting close to my goal at last.

I also sensed something else that I wasn't yet ready to admit. Everything I had heard during my search reinforced my belief that James hadn't left me for another woman. He'd spoken so fondly of me and our life together wherever he went that I was convinced that infidelity was not behind his disappearance. But that left only one other option: Something had happened to him . . .

As soon as I set foot in the inn in Bedford County, I knew my journey was almost at an end. I could picture James and Solomon here. Their presence was so tangible that I nearly called out to them as I followed the innkeeper's wife up to my room.

After freshening up a bit, I went down to the main dining area for supper. I listened with one ear to the local residents as they sat at the bar and discussed events. I had just started eating a piece of delicious apple pie when they started talking about the black dog that haunted the pass in the next county. My head jerked up and my hand started to shake so hard that I had to put down my fork. A black dog? Solomon was a black dog.

Apparently the black dog appeared every night at the same spot near the top of the pass. It walked back and forth along the trail as if it were guarding something. Folks traveling across the pass swore the beast was a ghost. Some claimed to have watched it pacing all night long, only to vanish with the sun's first light. According to the locals at the bar, a group of young rowdies once went to the haunted pass to see the black dog. Their horses panicked every time they drew near the huge hound, and they were forced to spend the night on the trail, unable to leave until the dog vanished with the daylight. The next night they came back to the pass, determined to kill the black dog. But their bullets passed right through his spectral body and kicked up dust on the other side. Frightened, they bolted down the trail, never to return, while behind them the black dog kept pacing back and forth, back and forth.

By this time I had covered my face with my hands, nearly bent double with pain. It couldn't be. Oh, it couldn't be! The innkeeper's wife saw my distress and hushed the patrons at the bar as she came to my side. Thinking they were frightening me, she put her plump arm around me comfortingly as she tried to lead me away upstairs. But I stopped her. Staring up into her motherly eyes, I whispered: "I must see the dog. Please, take me to the dog."

I saw a sudden flicker of understanding in her eyes. She'd been working here when James had passed through years ago. But until that moment, she'd never connected the spectral black dog with the disappearance of my husband.

Her voice husky with suppressed emotion, she called her husband, grown-up son, and a few of the more reliable patrons and asked them to ride up to the pass with me at sunset the next evening to show me the black dog. When they heard my story, they agreed.

Before we left the next evening, she made sure I was wrapped up warm and gave me a flask of whisky—"just in case." She didn't specify in case of what, but we both knew.

The ride up the pass seemed to take forever, and yet it passed too quickly. The truth was at the top of the ridge. I knew it in my bones. We rounded a bend, and in the light of the rising moon, I saw Solomon solemnly pacing along the trail ahead of us. I closed my eyes for a long, sorrowful moment. Then I slid off my horse and called my dog.

Solomon stopped abruptly and turned his great black head toward me. Then he let out a single bark of greeting and ran down the path toward me. My legs gave out and I sat down abruptly on the dirt of the path as Solomon loped up to me. When he reached me, he laid his head on my lap and moaned, just like he used to back home in England when he wanted something. I embraced him, though my arms met spectral cold where once was warm flesh.

"Where's James, Solomon?" I whispered. "Take me to James."

At once, my huge hound rose and started up the path, pausing a few feet away to make sure I was following. Behind me stalked a cadre of frightened but protective Virginia men, wanting to make sure I was safe. Solomon stopped suddenly beside a large rock at the edge of the trail. He pawed it anxious and gave a long wail of grief. Then he vanished.

With tears streaming down my cheeks, I asked the innkeeper and his son to dig at the spot indicated by the ghost of my faithful dog. After borrowing picks and shovels from a local resident, it did not take them long to uncover the remains of a huge hound and, buried beneath it, the bones of my husband— his signet ring still on his finger. There was no sign of his purse, and we assumed he must have been robbed and slain up there on the lonely pass not long after leaving Bedford County. The robbers had killed Solomon too. Our dog was very protective and would have tried to rip out the throat of anyone attacking my husband.

We took them both back to the inn, and the local minister held a lovely funeral for my husband and his dog. I wept as he spoke of the faithfulness of Solomon, who had kept his vigil even after death, until at last he could reunite his two beloved humans.

And then, at long last, it was over. I had found the truth, and as the Good Book said, it had set me free. I could move on with my life now, and I realized in that moment that my life was not here. I did not belong in Virginia. My family was in England, and that was where I would return.

So I booked passage home, spending my last night in America with Alicia and her husband. I told my faithful friends the whole story and showed them James's signet ring, which I wore around my neck.

"Does Solomon still haunt the pass?" Alicia asked as we parted for the night.

I shook my head. "The innkeeper's son went up to the pass at sunset to watch for him one night before the funeral, but he never appeared."

"His job was done," said Alicia's husband. "Now he can rest in peace."

Yes. Now he can rest.

And may you rest in peace, my Solomon, I thought as I readied myself for bed. And thank you for watching over my James so faithfully.

Jack Ma Lantern

When the new preacher moved to town, the members of his new congregation were quick to tell him about the Jack Ma Lantern that was haunting the roads out by the swamp. The preacher listened to all the stories the townsfolk told him about the evil spirit, but he just laughed to himself over them stories. He didn't believe in the Jack Ma Lantern.

Now that there Jack Ma Lantern was a bad spirit, shore 'nuff. He done so much evil in his lifetime that God didn't want nothing to do with him. Then he went and messed with the Devil too! He tricked ol' Nick twice, Jack did. He forced the Devil to give him another couple years of life, even though his time was up. That made the Devil real mad. So when Death came fer Jack Ma Lantern, not only did the good Lord toss him outta heaven but the Devil wouldn't let him into hell neither. So Jack had to wander the earth with a piece of brimstone fer a lantern. He was so darned mad about it that he spent all his time trying to kill off all the good folks that done right in this world, on account of they was going to heaven and he was stuck here on earth.

JACK MA LANTERN

The new preacher told his congregation that they were imagining that the Jack Ma Lantern haunted the swamp. They were seeing some sort of mist or reflected starlight on the water. It weren't nothing to be afraid of. Besides, they had the Lord on their side. All they had to do was pray and any evil spirits lurking about would have to leave them alone.

The congregation listened closely to the new preacher and thought he might be right about that Jack Ma Lantern. Then again, he might be wrong, him being new to the area and all. So they kept turning their pockets inside out when they walked down the road near the swamp, 'cause that was supposed to keep the Jack Ma Lantern away. And most folks avoided the road at night if they could. No use tempting fate.

At first, the preacher treated the whole story like a joke. But as the months passed, he became more an' more cross whenever he heard folks talking about the Jack Ma Lantern. He'd give a little hop of rage if he saw anybody walkin' around with their pockets turned inside out. Seemed to him like they was following heathen ways instead of trustin' God to protect them from evil.

The preacher started preaching almost every week about how silly it was to be afraid of the Jack Ma Lantern. All the folks in the congregation would say "Amen" and "Preach it, brother," but they still avoided the swamp road and walked around with their pockets inside out. And the folks that lived closest to the swamp sometimes wore *all* their clothes inside out, hopin' this would confuse the Jack Ma Lantern and he'd leave them alone.

One Saturday evening the preacher was reading his Bible out on the front porch when he saw Sister Evelyn passin' by with all her clothes inside out. Well, that done it!

"Sister Evelyn, why are your clothes inside out?" the preacher asked sternly, standing tall on the steps of his porch and waving his Bible at her.

Sister Evelyn gave a hunted look around, hoping for inspiration, but she didn't see anything that might help her appease the preacher. Afore she said a word, the preacher said, "You're scared of that silly Jack Ma Lantern, ain't ya? I told you the Lord would protect ya from evil spirits! All ya need is faith, Sister. Faith, not superstitions! You go home right now and put your clothes on right side out. And don't let me see you practicing heathen ways again!"

Sister Evelyn scurried home with her head down, glad the preacher couldn't see the silver coin in her pocket that she carried to keep away witches. And the preacher, he sat on the porch half the night brooding about the Jack Ma Lantern. It seemed that it was up to him to lay that story to rest, once and for all.

The next morning was Sunday. When the preacher got up into the pulpit, he announced to the whole congregation that he was gonna walk the swamp road that very night as the clock struck midnight, just to prove that the Jack Ma Lantern didn't exist. And when he got home in one piece, they were all to stop their heathen practices and trust in the Lord to protect them ever after.

The congregation exchanged worried looks with one another. "*If* ya get home, ya mean," muttered Brother Henry. He thought he spoke soft enough, but the preacher heard him and glared at him from the pulpit, giving a little hop of rage and waving his Bible for emphasis.

After church, folks crowded round the preacher and tried to give him their lucky amulets and silver coins. Brother Henry wanted him to take his best rabbit's foot that had garlic stuffed inside. But the preacher wouldn't take none of them heathen things.

"The Lord will protect me," he told them all. "The only thing I'm gonna take is the Holy Book. Y'all come to the swamp road tomorrow morning; you'll see me walkin' out of the swamp with my head held high and my clothes on right side out. And then y'all will know that the Jack Ma Lantern is just a fairy tale."

No one could talk the preacher out of his plan. So the congregation went home, shaking their heads. The preacher was a holy man of God, but that there Jack Ma Lantern, he was pure evil. No tellin' who would win this contest. No tellin' at all.

Right on the stroke of midnight, the preacher started walking down the swamp road, just like he promised. In one hand he carried a walking stick to test the marshy spots afore he stepped on them, and in the other he held his Bible. He'd spotted a big ol' fallen tree right in the middle of the swamp, and he planned to camp out there all night under the stars. In the morning he would walk back to the road to meet his repentant congregation and hold a prayer meeting right there on the swamp road. And that would be the end of the Jack Ma Lantern story.

As he drew near the swamp path leading to the big tree, the preacher thought he caught a glimpse of a light ahead of him.

Must be a reflection from the lantern at Sister Evelyn's place, he thought. *Strange that I can see it through all them trees.* Sister Evelyn's place was nearly a mile farther along the road. Still, lantern light did funny things at night.

From back in the swamp there came a hissing of the wind in the treetops. It almost sounded like words: "Jack (jack, jack). Jack (jack, jack)."

The preacher shivered a little and pulled his jacket tight around him. Fall was a-comin' early to these parts, he thought as he turned onto the path leading deeper into the swamp. The first few yards of the path were solid and dry, but it weren't long afore the ground started to wobble under the preacher's boots and he had to use his walking stick to make sure the ground was solid afore he stepped forward. Round about him, the wind whistled through the tall grass, swirling the fronds this way and that. They wrapped around the preacher's arms and legs like the misty hands of a ghost. Somewhere deep in the swamp, a voice hissed: "Jack (jack, jack). Jack (jack, jack)."

All the preacher's hair stood on end and he shuddered, clutching his Bible to his chest and raising the walking stick like a weapon. He strained his ears, listening intently to the whistle of the wind. A long cold finger of wind swept down his neck and under his collar. He gasped and shook. "Thi . . . is is nonsense," he muttered. "There ain't nobody here tonight but me and the Lord."

The wind rattled the bushes, and a light flickered somewhere off to the right. "Jack (jack, jack). Jack (jack, jack)," a sinister voice hissed softly under the rustling of the wind in the grass.

The preacher was shaking so hard that the wobbly ground under him made little splashing noises. "The Lord is with me!"

he shouted. His voice was caught by the sighing wind and disappeared within a few feet, but the words had unlocked the preacher's frozen knees. He stepped forward carefully, prodding the ground with his stick and mutterin' the Lord's Prayer to himself as he walked.

The wind died away and the sliver of moon disappeared behind a cloud. The swamp was plunged into a blackness that made the previous darkness seem like daylight. And with the darkness came an eerie silence that wrapped around the preacher until the only thing that he could hear was the slish-slosh of watery ground under his boots and the sound of his own breath.

The preacher felt his heart thumping mighty fiercely against his ribs. He wished—oh, how he wished—that he'd already reached the fallen tree and had its firm trunk against his back. *Anything* could be out here with him—anything at all. Suddenly the Jack Ma Lantern stories didn't sound so ridiculous.

A light appeared among the scattered trees to his right, lighting up a long, low pool of water filled with reeds. The light blinked on . . . off . . . on . . . off. "Jack (jack, jack)," an evil voice hissed softly. "Jack (jack, jack)."

The preacher fumbled for the pockets in his jacket and hastily turned them inside out. He felt guilty for doin' such a heathen thing, but fear overcame his guilt. Something was out here with him. Even with a Bible clutched to his chest, he didn't feel safe.

His knees were shaking so hard that they knocked together as he carefully moved forward through the swamp, sayin' the Lord's Prayer aloud as he walked. Behind him, a light appeared. The preacher whirled round to face it with a shriek. The light hovered over the soggy pathway, and little sparkles of light danced invitingly on the waters of a deep pool at the edge of the trail. Shakily, the preacher raised his walking stick and shouted: "Go away, in the name of God!"

Directly behind him, a sinister voice hissed in his ear: "Jack (jack, jack). Jack (jack, jack)."

Slivers of ice ran along the preacher's skin. He whirled round with a scream, slashing at his stalker with his walking stick. The walking stick passed right through the glowing, emaciated form looming in the path beside him. The round face was bone white, and the eyes were like two glowin' red coals.

"Jack (jack, jack)," the creature howled. "Jack (jack, jack)."

The preacher staggered backward, tripped over a weedy hummock, and nearly pitched headlong into the deep pool. He was saved when his jacket caught on a splinter of wood sticking out from a rotting stump at the edge of the water. Desperate, he yanked free just as the ghost light faded, leaving the path in darkness. The preacher gasped in panic. The spirit of the Jack Ma Lantern could be anywhere. Anywhere! But if he ran, he'd for sure fall into a pool and drown!

"Jack (jack, jack)," hissed a sinister voice right above his head.

The preacher stuttered out the words of the Lord's Prayer as he pulled off his jacket and turned it inside out. A bright light burst into being directly above his head. Crouching by the stump, the preacher opened his Bible and covered his face with it. He felt ghostly hands pluckin' at his boots, at his legs. Each touch was so cold it burnt his skin, right through his clothes.

"Jack (jack, jack)," hissed the Jack Ma Lantern. "Jack (jack, jack)."

"The Lord will protect me!" the preacher screamed from underneath the Bible plastered against his face. "The Lord will protect me!"

Suddenly there came the rumble of wagon wheels and a blaze of torch lights from the swamp road. A chorus of men's voices shouted an answer to the preacher's screams. The ghost light disappeared as men from the congregation swarmed up the swamp path to the place where the preacher crouched beside a dark pool. They carried torches in their hands and wore their clothes inside out, and their pockets jingled with all the amulets and silver coins they could hold.

Brother Henry was the leader of the group. He tried to rouse the tremblin' preacher, but he lay under his Bible in a stupor of absolute terror. He wouldn't move. The men were forced to carry him down the swamp path and out to the road, where they tucked him into the back of the wagon with the hay bales.

When he finally woke hours later, the preacher babbled madly about ghosts and evil spirits and glowin' red eyes. He tore all his clothes off—to the dismay of the ladies of the church who attended him—and tried unsuccessfully to turn them inside out. It took several men to restrain him, and the doc was forced to give him something to make him sleep again.

The doc did everything he could to save the preacher, but in the end he was sent to a home for insane folks. Every day for the rest of his life, he babbled to the attendants about the evil Jack Ma Lantern and screamed every time he saw a bright light.

No one goes near that swamp no more, and the swamp road is overgrown so bad that no one can travel there again. Which is a mercy.

25

Kitty

A long time ago, a young man came to Smyth County to earn his living. He worked very hard and saved every penny he made, and soon he had enough money to buy himself a farm. He had all his neighbors in to help him raise a house and a barn, and he stocked that barn with cows and pigs and horses and sheep. The young man was very good looking, but he had no wife to live with him on his very prosperous farm; his evenings were lonesome indeed.

One night, as he was sitting by the fireside eating his bowl of stew, a pretty little cat nudged her way into the house through a small, cat-size hole in the door. She came over to the young man and rubbed against his legs, purring to beat the band. He stroked her silky head and called her "my pretty." The cat spent the whole evening with him by the fireside, and he told her all about his day. She was good company, meowing and purring in all the right places and blinking her slanted green eyes beguilingly, just as if she were a human being. The young man was very sorry when she slipped out through the cat-size hole and went away.

KITTY

The young man thought about the cat the next day as he tended his livestock and other chores. He wondered if she would come back to the hearth that evening. He rather hoped she would.

The young man was just settling down to eat his supper when a pink nose appeared in the cat-size hole, followed swiftly by the whiskers, slanted green eyes, and overlarge ears of the pretty little cat. A moment later she was rubbing against his legs and he was offering her part of his supper, which she daintily accepted. Again they spent a quiet evening before the fire, and the young man told the cat all the funny little things that had happened throughout the day: the horse that made funny faces when he brushed it; the mother duck that hid her ducklings in the bull rushes; the big ram that kept getting his horns stuck in the thicket bush because he was too stubborn to go around it. The little cat purred and trilled little cat comments in all the right places, blinking her slanted green eyes beguilingly. The young man watched her leave with sadness and wondered if he might keep the pleasant little creature as a pet. If she came back, he would try.

He watched and waited the next evening as dinner cooked on the stove. As soon as he took his place at the hearthside table, the little cat appeared in the cat-size crack in the door and came inside, purring and rubbing against his legs as usual. Immediately the young man got up and nailed a board across the hole in the door, trapping the little cat inside with him. She gave a funny little mew and pawed unhappily at the boarded-up hole. But the young man picked her up and began rubbing her back soothingly, saying, "I just want you to stay here with me, little kitty."

As he spoke, the little cat gave a sigh that sounded almost human. And then she turned to mist in his hands. When the mist solidified, he found a very beautiful girl leaning against his side, staring at him through beguiling, slanted green eyes.

One look at this lovely lady was enough to topple the young man head over heels into love. She was even more wonderful than the cat. The young man talked and talked to the pretty girl, who nodded and smiled and hummed softly in her throat as if she were purring.

The next morning, the young man took his girl to the local preacher and married her. She was the sweetest little wife any man could wish for. She had a low, musical voice like the trill of a cat and a lovely way of humming when something pleased her. She answered to the name of Kitty, and everyone in the surrounding countryside loved her to pieces.

The young man and his Kitty had two little boys, one right after the other. They were sprightly young lads right from the start and had the same winning ways as their mother.

The little boys were about four and two years old on the night a huge storm blew into the valley where the young man and Kitty made their home. The trees in the valley bent double in the fierce wind. Mighty thunderheads filled the sky, and soon lightning was flashing everywhere. The young man brought all the livestock into the barn just in time. The heavens opened up as he barred the barn door, and it was pouring down rain when he ran to the house.

The young man was barely inside when the family heard shouts over the roar of the wind and rain. A carriage holding two couples had driven up to their door, and the folks inside came tumbling out, soaking wet and miserable with cold. Kitty ran to open the door and welcomed the poor travelers inside while the young man helped the two husbands unhitch the shying horses and led them to the barn.

"The Devil's in this storm," gasped one of the young women as she steamed herself dry before the fire. "It came up so sudden!"

The other woman nodded fervently, still too spent to speak.

The two little boys watched the strangers from the kitchen doorway, too shy to come out. Kitty set them gently aside so that she could bring the women steaming mugs of tea. They drank it gratefully and settled themselves in chairs by the very hearth that had first drawn the pretty little cat to the house so many years before.

When the men came in, Kitty brought them hot drinks and then served everyone a delicious stew with dumplings in it. Outside, the storm howled, and huge gusts of wind shook the house from top to bottom. But inside, the unexpected guests grew warm and dry and merry, and the little boys listened wide eyed to the tales they told of their travels. The men were brothers who married sisters, and they were honeymooning together, traveling wherever fancy took them through Virginia.

The young man asked each couple how they met and courted, listening to their stories with a dreamy look on his face. Kitty listened too, her face distant in the firelight. She drew her sons to her side, holding them close to her as the visitors talked loudly over the occasional crash of thunder and gust of wind. Her eyes strayed every once in a while to the small cat-size hole in the door that was covered by the board. The board had grown loose over the years but had never quite fallen off.

And then it was their turn to speak. The young man beamed when the visitors asked how he met his wife, and he began talking about the pretty little cat that often came to the fireside to spend the evening with him. Kitty tensed as he spoke, her eyes on the little cat-size hole in the door. Would he? Oh, would he?

When he reached the place in the story where he decided to trap the cat in the house so he could keep her as a pet, the young man went over to the door and gestured toward the board as he demonstrated what he had done. His hand bumped the loose wood as he spoke and the loose board swayed and then fell off the door, revealing the cat-size hole it had covered for so many years.

At that moment, a huge gust of wind shook the house from roof to foundation. And in the place where Kitty and her two sons had sat now appeared a pretty little cat with slanted green eyes and two small kittens—the spell that had trapped them in human form broke with the removal of the board.

The young man's mouth dropped open, and he stared at the cats in shock. Then he reached frantically for the board lying on the floor beside his boots. But before his hand closed around it, the three cats raced to the door and scampered through the cat-size hole and out into the storm.

"No!" screamed the young man. "Kitty, no!"

He wrenched open the door and leapt out into the storm, screaming his wife's name over and over again. The young man searched every nook and cranny on the farm in the mud and pouring rain. The visitors finally forced him to come inside before he caught pneumonia, but he was up at dawn the next morning. He searched the whole valley—the whole county—

for his wife and sons, calling their names over and over, half mad with grief.

But the cats were never seen again.

The young man died not long after his family disappeared into the storm. His once prosperous farm fell into ruin, and eventually the woods overran it completely. There's nothing there now but a few rotted boards and an old chimney. Some say if you visit the place just before or after a storm, you can hear the young man's voice echoing through the hills and valleys of his old home, crying "Kitty! Kitty! Kitty!"

Fire!

RICHMOND

It was so exciting! The opening of *The Bleeding Nun* at the theater on Broad Street was taking place the day after Christmas this year of 1811, and I was going. My husband, bless his heart, thought I was crazy. I could talk of nothing else for days—the famous actress who had a leading role; the rumor that the governor was going to attend the opening. So many of Richmond's rich and famous would be attending—a veritable *Who's Who* of Virginia—and I had a ticket!

My husband absolutely hates the theater and refused to go with me, so I was invited to attend with a group of our neighbors. It was this circumstance that cast the first pall over the occasion for me. Oh, it was not my neighbors themselves who dampened my enthusiasm for the evening. They were very friendly, and I often took tea with Mrs. Gibson and Mrs. McRae. In fact, that's what we were doing the day of the play, drinking holiday tea and discussing the evening's entertainment, when Nancy Green, Mrs. Gibson's young ward, came racing into the room in an utter panic. Her face was pale with anxiety, her hair windblown and her eyes so huge that I could see myself reflected in them.

FIRE!

"Why, Nancy, what is wrong?" Mrs. Gibson asked. And the girl, shaking from head to toe, stuttered out her story.

She had been visiting a shop on Broad Street and was returning home by way of Eighth Street, which crossed a ravine, when she sensed something was wrong.

"The air went all funny," the girl gasped.

"What do you mean the air went all funny?" Mrs. Gibson asked.

"It started to shimmer a bit, like it does on real hot days. Only the wind coming from the ravine was real cold," Nancy explained, pulling her cloak tight around her for comfort as she spoke. "It made me shake under my cloak. I felt real scared, like someone was watching me, so I started to hurry along the street, keeping away from the ravine, which was filled with dark shadows."

Nancy swallowed nervously and stared out of the window into the twilit garden. I thought she was pale before, but now she went white and trembled visibly. "One of the shadows kept pace with me along the road, staying with me even when I walked real fast. I was so scared; I didn't know what to do. And then the whole world twisted a little. The wind swirled around me like a whirlwind, the shimmering air encircled me so that I had to stop in my tracks or fall over. I found myself facing the ravine, and the writhing dark shadow was right in front of me. I tried to scream, but there was a huge lump in my throat. All I could do was stand there and shake. And then a voice called to me from the horrible specter."

Her voice grew shriller and faster as she spoke, and her last few words choked off as if a hand had been clapped over her mouth. She clutched at her throat, swallowing heavily, and Mrs.

Gibson got up from her chair and put a comforting arm around her ward's shoulders.

"What did the voice say, Nancy?" she asked kindly.

Nancy, pale as a ghost herself, whispered: "It s-said . . . it said, 'Nancy . . . Nancy . . . Nancy Green. You'll die before you are sixteen.'"

The girl's knees buckled then, and Mrs. Gibson helped her to a chair. I swallowed hard and shoved my teacup away from me, as if the act could shove away the girl's horrible story. Nancy's sixteenth birthday was tomorrow.

Mrs. Gibson poured the girl a cup of tea and started trying to talk some sense into her.

"I'm sure you imagined the whole thing, Nancy," Mrs. Gibson said soothingly. "There are no such things as ghosts. You've heard your foster father say that many times, and it is true."

"I know what I heard," Nancy muttered into her teacup, refusing to meet Mrs. Gibson's eyes. "I want to stay home tonight. I don't want to go to the play."

Nancy kept insisting that she wanted to stay home that night until Mrs. Gibson told her sharply that proper respect for her father demanded her presence at the play. That stopped the girl in her tracks. She loved her foster father very much and would do anything to please him. Besides, he had paid a great deal of money for the theater tickets, and it would be a terrible waste if she did not go. So Nancy assented to attend the theater with us. Relieved by this return to sensibility, Mrs. Gibson sent her to her room to dress for the evening's activities.

I glanced over to Mrs. McRae, who had been watching the scene with eyes nearly as large as Nancy's had been when she first came into the room. I didn't blame the girl for wanting to stay safely at home. But I also thought Mrs. Gibson was right to scold her for saying that she didn't want to go to the play. Tickets were expensive, and a night out at the theater would drive the whole scary experience right out of the girl's head. She probably *had* imagined the whole incident. I'd walked along Eighth Street many times, right next to the "spooky" ravine, and there was nothing remotely frightening there. The child had probably been hearing scary stories from her friends and was shying at shadows because of it.

It was time for all of us to dress for the theater, and Mrs. McRae and I went to our respective homes. I still felt a bit spooked by the girl's story and repeated it to my husband when I went to show him the new dress I'd bought for the occasion.

My husband looked a little dubious when I finished the tale. "I think I'm with Nancy on this one," he said. "I'm not sure I want you to go to the theater this evening."

Not go to the play? When the elite of Virginia society would be there? It was unthinkable!

"I'll be fine," I told him firmly. "I'm sure the girl imagined the whole thing."

And so we went to the theater that night. Oh, it was a gala affair. Everyone was laughing, chatting, and greeting acquaintances home for the Christmas holiday. The house was packed with people in elegant clothing from pit to balcony. I saw the governor looking magnificent and a little stern as he made his way to his box. There was standing room only, and we were lucky to have seats in the balcony.

I sat between Mrs. McRae and Mrs. Gibson, and Nancy sat on the far side of us with the rest of our party. The play was enthralling, and I was sorry when it ended. After a brief intermission, everyone reassembled in the theater to see the pantomime that came next. I quite enjoyed the first act and was eagerly watching an actor declaiming his piece in the "den of robbers" at the start of the second when Mrs. Gibson nudged me in the ribs and gestured toward the curtain at the back. Thick black smoke was rising toward the ceiling, and I thought I saw the flicker of flames.

"Is it part of the play?" I whispered to her, my pulses giving a slight leap of alarm.

"I'm not sure," Mrs. Gibson whispered back.

And then a man came out onto the stage, interrupting the play with words that made my body go rigid with fear: "The house is on fire!" At that moment, sparks and flames rained down over the stage, right on top of the actors.

The cry of "Fire!" passed with electric velocity through the theater as everyone flew from their seats. "Stay with me, Nancy," Mrs. Gibson cried, taking her ward by the hand. Mrs. McRae and I clung together as we tried to push our way through the panicking crowds toward the narrow staircase that led down to the library. But our seats were at the top of the house, and already the stairs were jammed with frantic, screaming people fleeing from the pit. To my horror, I saw a little girl trampled to death beneath unheeding feet. I screamed for people to stop, but no one heard me over the roar of the rapidly spreading fire, which was already licking the walls of the theater. Several of the bolder patrons actually leaped from the balcony down into the pit, but most of them were swallowed into the seething mass of people and probably also trampled to death.

Thick, acrid smoke filled the theater, making me cough violently. Someone elbowed me in the ribs so fiercely that I screamed and doubled in pain. In the chaos of shoving bodies, crying children, and weeping adults, I got separated from both Mrs. Gibson and Mrs. McRae. I forced my way forward, careful to stay on my feet lest I too be trampled. But by now the pine boards of the roof, full of resin, had caught and the place was like a bonfire. The staircase down from the balcony was so full of people that I knew I'd never make it out that way.

I started pushing my way against the crowd, heading toward the walls at the back of the balcony. There had to be another way out. With stinging eyes and gasping for breath, I searched through black smoke for a window, bent almost double to reach the clearer air under the smoke. The fire was everywhere, and the heat was appalling. Sweat dripped off me, and my ears rang with the shrieks of those who were dying or searching for lost loved ones. It sounded like a frenzied funeral dirge—my funeral dirge.

I reached the wall; there was no crowd here, but there *was* fire, licking its way down from the roof. I dodged the worst of it and kept beating at the sparks that landed on my fancy dress. I could smell my hair burning, and I beat at that too with one hand while I searched for a window. The roar of the fire was like a maddened beast. The sound made my whole body tremble in fear.

Then ahead of me I saw Mrs. McRae framed in an open window and heard a familiar voice urging her to jump. Half staggering, half crawling, my body shaking with the pain of my burns and the terrible bruise on my ribs, I reached the window as Mrs. McRae jumped into the arms of my husband below.

Seeing me peering out the window, he set Mrs. McRae safely on the ground and ran back to the burning theater.

"Jump, darling! Jump," he screamed. And I jumped.

That moment is burned into my brain for all eternity. I was airborne, with sparks, flickering flames, and acrid black smoke all around me. A cold winter breeze touched my cheeks, a strange sensation amidst the burning heat of the fire. I could see Mrs. McRae sitting on the ground and a crowd milling outside the theater. Below me was the frantic face of my beloved husband, pale in the ghastly firelight.

My fall lasted an eternity . . . and two seconds. And then I landed in my husband's arms with a thump that rattled my broken rib. He dropped at once to the ground and rolled both of us over and over to put out the fire in my hair and dress. Rising, he escorted the terrified Mrs. McRae and me to the nearest medic to have our wounds dressed and then took us both home. As soon as he was sure I was safely in the hands of my maid, my husband went back to help put out the fire.

In all, seventy-two persons died that night in the fire, fifty-four of them women. My dear friend Mrs. Gibson was one of them and so was her ward, Nancy Green, who did *not* live to be sixteen.

Foul Smell

ALEXANDRIA

We were doing a marathon drive from south Florida to our house in Maine the last week of June, and when we hit Virginia I was done.

"Let's look for a place to spend the night," I said to my husband as we passed the "Welcome to Virginia" sign.

"Nah, it's still early," he protested. "Let's get up to D.C. before we quit for the day."

"Well, I'm done driving. You want to keep going, you've got the wheel," I said crisply, turning off the highway and pulling into a fast-food place. We grabbed a couple of burgers and sodas before heading back onto the road, this time with my husband driving.

It was very late when we got within shouting distance of Washington, D.C. The first few hotels we tried were booked up—there was some kind of conference in town. We finally found a little motel way off the beaten path, and even they had only one room left.

It wasn't the prettiest room—just a bed, a seedy-looking desk, an old armchair, and a dresser with a TV on it. Still, we were just here for eight hours. It would do.

FOUL SMELL

I jumped into the shower to get some hot-water therapy for the kinks driving had put into my back. The shower was clean, at least, if teeny. I could barely turn around without hitting the curtain. In the bedroom I heard my husband turn on the TV. He's addicted to sports and needed his fix before he could sleep.

It wasn't until I hurried out of the warm bathroom and jumped into bed in my nice clean jammies that I noticed a strange smell. The odor was icky sweet and rotten, like something bloody and decaying. It turned my stomach.

"Yuck! What's that smell?" I said, sitting bolt upright and fanning the air in front of my nose. From that position, the foul smell faded a bit.

"I don't smell anything," said my husband, who was slumped in the faded armchair by the window. "Maybe a little dust."

"This ain't dust," I snapped. "Come here and take a whiff."

My husband flicked off the TV and came to the bed. As soon as he leaned down, his face crinkled in the most awful grimace. "Eeww!" he said. "It smells like a dead cat! I'm calling the front desk."

He picked up the phone, motioning for me to get out of the bed. "Don't stay in there, honey. There might be germs or something."

I jumped out of bed and hurried into the bathroom to put on my robe while my husband bullied the fellow at the front desk into coming up to the room with some air freshener and a vacuum cleaner.

"A vacuum cleaner?" I asked from the bathroom.

"Maybe it's bedbugs," said my husband.

That freaked me out. Bedbugs? Yuck! I did a little "bedbug removal" dance: wiggling and twisting to make sure there weren't any bedbugs crawling over me. Double yuck! The dance brought me close to the bed again, and I caught another whiff of the dead-cat smell. My stomach lurched and I raced back to the bathroom, sure I was going to be sick.

By the time my poor stomach was back under control, the fellow from the front desk was knocking at the door. He came in with an expression that said quite clearly that he was not happy with our late-night complaint.

"What smell are you talking about?" he asked, taking a big sniff as soon as he stepped inside. "I don't smell nothing but dust."

"Over by the bed," my husband said. "Smells like something died over there. You may want to check underneath."

The desk clerk gave my husband a disbelieving look and marched over to the bed, dragging the vacuum cleaner behind him. But he recoiled as soon as he leaned over. Looking a little queasy, he backed away. "I'm sorry, folks. I had no idea it was so bad."

The desk clerk poked the vacuum cleaner hose under the bed, but it went in only a few inches. He knelt down and picked up the dust ruffle. "Bed frame goes all the way to the floor," he announced, standing up and waving his hand in front of his nose.

I thought he was going to lose his dinner right then and there, but he swallowed a couple of times and managed to regain some color in his pale cheeks. "It must be something in the bedsprings," he said. "Maybe a mouse ate its way inside and died there. Can you help me move the mattress, sir?"

A mouse? Personally I was sure it was bedbugs, and my skin crawled at the thought.

My husband grabbed the top of the mattress and the desk clerk grabbed the bottom. They shoved the mattress aside, pulling it toward the window. The mattress temporarily blocked their view, so I was the first one to see the cause of the terrible smell.

I screamed.

Underneath the mattress, the box spring had been hollowed out. Twisted grotesquely inside it was the rancid, decaying figure of a woman in a bloodstained dress. Her glassy eyes stared blindly up at me, and her throat was cut from ear to ear. I screamed again and again, unable to take my eyes off the horrible sight. My husband had to shake me to get me to stop.

We spent the rest of the night reporting the incident to the police and filling out forms down at the station. Thankfully, it was quickly ascertained that the body had been in the box spring for more than a week, so we weren't under suspicion ourselves. After leaving a full itinerary with the police so that they could find us if they needed to, my husband and I headed back out onto the road.

"No more seedy hotels," my husband said grimly once we'd shaken the dust of that horrible place off our feet. "The next time we travel anywhere, we are making reservations in advance."

"At a four-star hotel," I said firmly.

And my husband agreed.

28

Trail of Blood

GLOUCESTER

It was one of those tragedies that could have been avoided. But fate—in the form of the master of the household—was too proud and too stubborn. And it cost him his daughter.

We all loved little Elizabeth. She was pretty and spirited and friendly with all the staff, just a wonderful child. And she was so lovely when she grew up that it took your breath away to look at her. Her father was so proud. He took her to England to show her off to the world. And that's where the trouble began, for Elizabeth fell in love with a handsome young gentleman she met there.

Elizabeth told me all about him the day she got home. I'd been Elizabeth's ladies maid when she lived at home and resumed the role upon her return. While I was brushing out her long hair that night, she bubbled on and on about her young man. They were engaged to be married. The final arrangements were to arrive by letter, and then they would be wed. Elizabeth was ecstatic.

But day after day passed, and then week after week, and no letter arrived. Elizabeth pounced on the mail every day, only to be disappointed. She began to pine, losing her color and

TRAIL OF BLOOD

moping about the house. She stopped going to parties and local events, and even her beloved father could not get her to smile.

"She will be fine," he said briskly when questioned about her condition. "It's just a minor infatuation. All girls go through it. Myself, I never liked the lad."

Indeed, I found out later that the Master hated the gentleman who'd won his daughter's heart and had intercepted and burned every letter the suitor had written to Elizabeth. But at the time, I believed—as did my young mistress—that the English gentleman had abandoned her.

It was a cold autumn, and I wasn't surprised when Elizabeth, weakened by sorrow, caught a chill. She became quite ill, and nothing the doctor did seemed to help. After several nights of restlessness and high fever, she suddenly grew cold and stopped breathing. I was stricken when I brought her lunch upstairs and found that she was gone.

Everyone in the household mourned the death of such a lovely young girl. Her father went ashen when he heard of her death. It was obvious that he blamed himself.

It was a cold, windy day in November when family, friends, and servants gathered in the garden to lay poor Elizabeth to rest. I wept bitterly and could not be comforted. I'd learned just that afternoon of her father's treachery regarding the English suitor. I was furious with him—and with myself. I should have probed deeper into the matter. If I had, I could have comforted my mistress—perhaps mailed a letter to her suitor for her or intercepted one of his missives myself. But I had believed the father's story, and only now that it was too late were my eyes opened to the truth.

On the other side of the open grave stood the family butler, who had told me about the Master's scheme against his daughter. He was glaring bitterly at the Master, who stood with his head bowed in grief as the minister spoke the eulogy. The butler wasn't upset about Elizabeth's death or the Master's treachery. No, he was angry over some slight one of the family members had given him that morning. To me it was a trifling thing compared with the tragic death of the daughter of the family, but he could not forget it.

Later I heard him in the kitchen, complaining to the cook about all the valuable jewelry that had been buried with my young mistress. "First they insult me, and then they waste all that money on a dead woman," he said loudly.

"Hush," the cook said, nervously glancing about. "The Master will not tolerate such talk."

"The Master! The Master!" the butler said, his face turning beat red. "I'll tell you what I think of the Master." He started swearing then, using words I'd never heard before and didn't care to know the meaning of. I clapped my hands over my ears and fled from the room, shocked at such behavior.

I sought refuge in the young mistress's rooms, saying good-bye as I sadly put her lovely clothing away for the last time. I stayed up late, tidying things in order to ease some of my grief. Finally everything was in its place. As I turned to leave, I saw a light flashing in the garden. Curious, I glanced outside and saw the butler stalking down the garden toward the family graveyard carrying a lantern. The sight made me uneasy. *He must be on an errand for the Master,* I thought. But my skin prickled as I remembered his words in the kitchen.

Instead of going to bed, I made my way downstairs and mentioned what I'd seen to one of the footmen and then to the cook, who was washing up the last of the dishes. "I'm sure he's doing something for the Master," Cook said reassuringly. "He was just talking nonsense before to relieve his feelings. I wouldn't worry about it, my dear."

Somewhat reassured, I made my way upstairs. As I silently passed the Master's study, I caught a glimpse of him through the open door. He was standing in front of a roaring fire, his face grim and sad. *Good,* I thought bitterly. He should be feeling remorse after what he'd done to Elizabeth. Outside, the wind picked up and I caught a glimpse of snowflakes piling up against the window beside the Master. I shivered, imagining my poor cold mistress buried under the snow. Tears poured down my cheeks as I hurried upstairs to my bedroom in the garret.

I paused on the landing for a moment and glanced out the window to see if I could spot the butler going about his errand for the Master. I still felt terribly uneasy, in spite of Cook's words. I glimpsed a faint light glowing in the family graveyard and thought for a moment that I heard a shout of alarm. But it may have only been the wind gusting against the house as the snow began falling in earnest.

I went to bed but couldn't sleep. After tossing and turning for nearly an hour, I rose, dressed, and went down to the kitchen for a drink of water. Cook was still there, sitting in front of the fire with her cup. She smiled when she saw me, a sympathetic smile. She knew how close I'd been to the young mistress. Her compassionate smile brought the tears again, and she held me close and let me weep until the rush of pain had passed. Then she made me drink a hot cup of tea.

"On your way upstairs, take this tray in to the Master. I know," she said, seeing the look on my face, "you don't approve of what he did. But he loved his daughter and thought he was doing the right thing. Don't you go judging the man so harshly. Think of how you'd feel someday if you thought your little girl was in love with a wrong one."

I blinked, struck by the thought. "I still wouldn't have interfered," I said defensively.

"Maybe you wouldn't, or maybe you would. Think about it," Cook advised.

I nodded slowly and picked up the tray. As I passed through the hall on my way to the study, I heard something scratching at the front door. *One of the dogs,* I thought as I knocked on the study door. The Master bade me enter, and I carried the tray over to a side table and set it down.

"Excuse me, Master," I said with a curtsy. "I heard one of the dogs scratching at the front door. Should I let it in?"

The Master shook his head, tearing his eyes away from the fire with effort. "The dogs can stay outside tonight. If they get cold, they can sleep in the barn."

"Very good, sir," I said with another curtsy. "Will there be anything else?"

He shook his head again. "No, Hannah, that will do."

I nodded and left the room. I could still hear a faint scratching at the door as I went back up the stairs for the third and final time that night. The poor dog just wanted in from the cold, but I couldn't disobey the Master. He said the dogs could sleep in the barn tonight, and that was that.

Cruel to his daughter and his dogs, I thought, trying to regain some of my anger from earlier that day. But Cook had

made me see the situation in a different light. Moreover, it was obvious the Master was suffering over the death of his beloved daughter. Life was hard to figure out. Wearily, I undressed and went back to bed.

I was awakened suddenly the next morning by a shrill scream coming from downstairs. I threw on a dressing gown and ran as fast as I could down to the front hallway. By the time I reached it, there was quite a crowd gathered at the open front door.

"What is the meaning of this?" roared the Master, wading into the huddle of gaping servants. I followed in his wake, anxious to see what all the fuss was about. Then I stopped abruptly with a gasp, my heart clutching within me. A figure lay huddled in a drift of snow on the doorstep—a familiar figure in a thin dress and bare feet. It was Elizabeth! One hand was stretched imploringly toward the front door, only inches from the wood. There was a bloody stump where one of her fingers had been cut off. A finger that, when she was buried, had borne an expensive ring. In a cold, detached way, I noticed that all the jewelry had been stripped from her body. By the butler, I suspected. But why had he dumped her body here? And how was it possible that her hand had bled so profusely after death?

Behind her dead body and stretching away toward the family graveyard, I could see a faint trail of blood in the snow. The marks indicated that someone had walked—no, had crawled—from the graveyard to the door. It was in that moment I realized the truth.

"Dear God, no!" I cried over the buzzing whispers of the other servants. "We buried her alive! We buried her alive!"

Elizabeth must have been roused from her deathlike stupor when the butler, who had obviously dug up her grave, had cut off her finger to steal the expensive ring it bore. It must have been his scream I heard when I peered out of the window on the landing last night. And that meant that the scratching I had heard at the door last night had not been the sound of a dog. It must have been . . . it had been . . .

I clapped my hand over my mouth and ran for the necessary, my stomach lurching. I crouched in the necessary and was sick over and over until there was nothing left to be sick with. And still I kept trying to throw up. They finally sent Cook in with some herbs to settle my stomach and then put me to bed for the rest of the day.

My conjectures were all confirmed while I lay ill in my bed. The butler was missing, the grave dug up. The lantern lay extinguished on its side in the new-fallen snow, and a long, wide trail dotted with blood indicated where Elizabeth had dragged herself out of the coffin and through the garden to the front door. There were even marks on the bottom of the door where her fingers had scratched at the wood trying to get in. In the end, she had frozen to death on the doorstep and been softly buried under an inch of snow.

Every time I thought about the scratching sound, I tried to be sick. The doctor finally put me to sleep with laudanum to stop the cycle of illness.

It was Cook who finally helped me cope with my pain. Taking me in her big arms, she shook me gently. "You aren't to blame," she said firmly. "None of us is to blame, except maybe the Master. And he thought he was doing what was best for his girl."

I stared at her mutely, unable to speak.

"I mean it, Hannah," Cook said. "She was dead and buried. None of us could have known what the sound at the door was. How could we guess such a thing? You are not to blame!"

I believed her finally, and from that moment I began to recover from my debilitating illness. But I couldn't stay at that house. Even the Master acknowledged that, and I was sent to work for another family. I never went back.

I heard later that a trail of blood leading from the family graveyard to the porch was seen each year after the first snowstorm—and that Elizabeth's ghost could be heard wandering around the house, tending to the fires and walking up the staircase. But I never went back to see.

Rupp

Pa's face was grim when he came into dinner that night.

"Someone's been messing with our cattle, Maude," he said to Mama. She looked up from the stove, her face flushed pink from the heat and little tendrils of curls hanging down into her eyes. She brushed them away impatiently.

"What do you mean?" she asked, catching up the kettle with a potholder and bringing it over to the table to pour into the teapot.

"Two of our cattle are down. And that's not the worst of it." He glanced at me as he spoke, and I straightened up indignantly. I was thirteen years old, practically a woman grown. If there was trouble coming our way, I was old enough to handle it, and I said so to Pa. His face softened a fraction, and he tousled my hair. Then he told us what he'd found.

Two of our cows had been dismembered in a back field. The head and hindquarters were all that remained of the cattle, and when Pa investigated the grisly remains, he found that they'd been drained of every drop of blood.

Mama went pale when she heard this. There was a story told in her family about a great aunt who'd died in mysterious

RUPP

circumstances over in Europe a long time ago. She too had been drained of blood, and her family thought she'd been killed by a vampire who'd been stalking young women in their town for several years.

We were all thinking about the story, but none of us said the word aloud. We didn't want to jinx ourselves, although I couldn't think of anything else that would drain all the blood out of a creature. I shuddered, and Pa patted my shoulder reassuringly.

"I'm sure there's a logical explanation for it," he said unconvincingly. "Maybe a bear got them."

"A bear that drinks blood?" There, I'd said it. Mama winced and turned away.

"Just you keep your window closed at night, Katie," Pa said, and that was that—end of conversation; end of mystery.

But it wasn't the end of the story. No, we'd only just begun.

Three days later our neighbor lost a cow under the same mysterious circumstances. Then a family on the other side of the ridge. And then a farmer on the far side of town. There were lots of foreigners around these days, men who had come from Europe to work in the mines. And they'd heard of vampires, just like we had, though I doubted any of them had lost family to one.

A few days later a number of prominent townsmen just "happened" to drop into the tavern after supper to discuss the matter. Most had lived in these parts all their lives, but there were a few newcomers too. All of them seemed above suspicion, though Mama made Pa carry garlic and a silver cross, just in case.

During the meeting, the names of several men were bandied about, all of them newcomers and all of them miners. Everyone seemed to think it was one of them behind the cattle killings. After all, the men went down into the mines before daylight and came up after dark—a perfect setup for a vampire. No one came to any conclusion that night, but when Pa got home he warned Mama and me to stay away from the mine, just in case.

My best friend Joshua, who lived next door, came over after chores the next afternoon to discuss the mysterious cattle killings. "I have an idea about that," he said importantly, swinging himself up onto the paddock fence and leaning his back against the post. "There's that weird fellow living on the other side of the ridge. Rupp he calls himself. He's a newcomer and he works in the mines. And no cattle went missing before he arrived."

I considered this. Rupp was a sort of neighbor of ours. We had to pass the turnoff to his remote cabin on our way to town. I'd only seen him once or twice, but each time something about him had frightened me. He was tall, thin, and very white of skin, with blood-red lips and narrow dark eyes. It was the look in those eyes that made me want to run away whenever I saw him. They had a hungry look that made my skin crawl. And the two times I'd seen him had both been at night. I'd never seen him during the day.

"Of course he's in the mine during the day," I said, continuing my thought out loud. Josh must have been following the expressions on my face, for he responded to my comment as if I'd spoke my previous thoughts aloud.

"He *says* he's in the mines during the day," he said. "We have no proof that he's really there."

"But don't they have to sleep in their coffins or something like that?" I asked, trying to remember the details about my great-aunt's supposed killer. "Rudd lives in a one-room cabin. A coffin would be pretty obvious."

"Not if it's up in the loft. I'm going to check," Josh said, slipping down off the fence post.

"I'm coming too," I said. Josh froze in his tracks and then turned, a fierce, protective look on his face.

"You are going to stay right here with your pa and mama," he said. "I don't want you anywhere near Rupp. Do you hear me?"

I was startled and flushed a little at the look on his face. A few times that spring, I'd wondered if Josh thought of me as more than a friend. Now I was certain.

"Promise me, Kate," he said sternly.

I promised.

"I'll take Fred along. Safety in numbers," he said. Fred was the neighbor on the other side of Josh. He was a big, strong lad a few years older than Josh and me. I nodded approvingly. They should be safe. I hoped.

We were sitting down to dinner when Josh and Fred came bursting into the kitchen.

"Rupp," Josh gasped, his eyes going straight to my father. "Rupp."

Fred grabbed my father by the arm, and the boys dragged him outside into the yard. Mama and I rushed to the window to watch and listen. The three of them stood by the paddock fence. We could hear their voices, but a storm was blowing up, and the wind whipped their words away before we could make them out. We saw Pa's face go grim, and then he left with the boys, heading toward town.

Mama told me to close all the windows and lock the doors. She got out the garlic and some of the holy amulets passed down in her family and draped them over us. Then we sat down in front of the fireplace and waited for Pa to come home.

It was late when we heard someone fumbling at the front door. We glanced at each other, bodies tensed. Then we heard a key in the lock and knew it was Pa. He came wearily in and saw our worried faces at once in the shadowy firelight.

"The boys looked through the cabin window and saw Rupp gnawing on a raw calf leg," he said without preamble. "We spoke to the sheriff about it, but he said it isn't against the law to eat raw meat. Folks in the tavern were pretty agitated by the sheriff's attitude, but his hands are tied, since there's no actual proof that the cow's leg came from one of the mutilated animals. No proof," he repeated, as if trying to convince himself. But the look on his face told us he was convinced that Rupp was behind the dead cattle.

Rumors buzzed around town for several days after Josh and Fred's visit to Rupp's cabin, but as the weeks passed without another dead cow, things settled down. Then the town drunk went missing. Of course he went missing twice a month, regular, right after he got a paycheck. But this was different. He was still a week shy of getting paid, and he hadn't shown up for several days. Finally the sheriff went looking for him and found his body in the valley a quarter mile below Rupp's cabin. He was drained of blood and missing an arm and a leg.

Unfortunately, Rupp's was not the only home near the valley where the murdered man was found. The sheriff had to question everyone who lived nearby, including us. Everyone denied knowledge of the murder, including Rupp, who didn't show up at his cabin until well after dark on the day the body was found. He spoke to the sheriff at length in the small clearing outside his cabin but did not invite him inside, and the sheriff couldn't force the issue without a search warrant, which he didn't have.

The sheriff stopped by our house after his interview with Rupp to talk to Pa, who was a good friend of his. The two men decided the sheriff should apply to the judge for a search warrant for Rupp's place, if only to dispel the rumors surrounding the man. It was at least a two-day trip and could take even longer if the judge wasn't home.

The sheriff headed out to the county courthouse the next morning, so he didn't hear about the traveling salesman who hadn't shown up to breakfast at the inn. The innkeeper's wife was alarmed when she went to make up his room and found the bed hadn't been slept in. The man's horse was still in the inn stable. But he was missing.

We heard all about it at school that day. Everyone discussed it over lunch and decided that the vampire must have gotten the salesman either right before or right after he talked to the sheriff. All the girls, even me, shuddered at the thought, and Josh boldly took my hand to comfort me. He held my hand all through lunch and smiled shyly at me as we parted at the school door to go to our separate desks.

I had to run a few errands in town for Mama after school, and I lingered too long in the grocery, looking longingly through the new book of dress patterns that had just arrived. It was dusk when I set off on the road home, my basket clenched at my side. The road was long and winding and already nearly dark in the shadow of the tall trees on either side. I kept remembering the story of the dismembered drunk and the missing salesman as I walked alone down the road. Normally the nighttime woods were my friend. But not now. Not since Rupp came.

I shuddered at the thought, remembering that I had to pass the lane leading toward Rupp's cabin. I quickened my pace, wanting to be well away from the spot before true darkness fell. I wished that I had asked Josh to come on my errands with me. But I knew he had chores to do, so I hadn't.

The wind whistled mournfully through the tops of the trees as I hastened down the darkening road. The smallest sounds made me jump: the rustle of small creatures in the underbrush, the hoot of a newly awakened owl, the raucous squawking of a crow. I hugged the basket close to me, walking as fast as I could. I saw Rupp's lane ahead and sped up until I was almost running. My eyes kept straying toward the sinister, overgrown lane—more of a deer trail than a proper road. And that's how I spotted the man's shoe sticking out of the underbrush a few yards down the lane.

I stopped suddenly, my whole body prickling with terror. *Oh, no,* I thought. *Please don't let it be the salesman.* I wanted to run for home, but I couldn't pass by without looking. What if it had been Pa who'd gone missing, or Josh? I'd have wanted to know.

I crept cautiously down the lane, the basket held in front of me like a shield. I parted the bush above the shoe, and a wave of nausea filled me as I spied the deathly white face and dismembered body of a man in a travel suit. I gasped, my whole body shaking in reaction to the sight. And then I froze as behind me a voice hissed, "Hello, little girl. What brings you here on this lovely night?"

It was Rupp.

I whirled with a shriek and pressed my back into the bush that held the salesman's body. "H . . . hello, Mr. Rupp," I whispered, holding the basket up between us. "I thought I saw something in the bushes, but it was j . . . just a trick of the light," I lied desperately.

The vampire's dark eyes glowed with a reddish glint in the dim twilight. His pale face was almost ruddy with the new blood he'd taken from his victim. It was obvious that he didn't believe my story. It was also obvious that I was not going to make it out of this situation alive. He smiled at me in the gloaming, and I saw two incisors slowly lengthen into sharp points as he raised his hands toward my throat.

And then another voice came from the main road: "Kate! Katie! Are you there?"

It was Josh, coming to look for me. His words were echoed immediately by a deeper man's voice. Pa.

"Here!" I screamed. "Here!"

Quick as a flash, Rupp disappeared into the woods beside me. So light on his feet was the vampire that I did not hear a rustle or a twig crack.

Pa and Josh came running into the lane, and I fell into their arms, babbling desperately about Rupp and the dead salesman in the bushes behind me. Pa took one look into the shrubbery and sent me home with Josh. I clung to my best friend, weeping and explaining how Rupp had appeared from nowhere and how he had reached for my throat. When I mentioned Rupp's elongated incisors, my voice went all to pieces and Josh looked rather murderous himself. He explained that they'd grown worried when I wasn't home by dusk and had come to look for me, knowing I'd have to pass Rupp's lane on my way home.

"Thank God we did," he added fervently, hugging me close to him.

Josh made sure I was safe in my mother's arms before he returned to town with Pa to see what the men meant to do about Rupp. Mama and I were preparing for bed when we heard shouts coming from the lane down the road. Rushing to an upper window, we saw through the trees the flickering light of torches heading toward Rupp's place. Not long after, we saw a massive fire reaching up and up to the sky and knew the vampire's cabin was burning.

Pa came in around midnight, and we both rushed downstairs to meet him.

"He's gone," Pa said, sinking wearily into a kitchen chair. "We searched everywhere, but he knew we'd be after him after he threatened Kate, and he bolted. The cabin was full of blood and gore and dismembered body parts—some of them human."

Pa's face went a bit green at the memory, and for a moment I was afraid he'd lose his dinner. But he recovered after a moment and went on: "Search parties scoured the woods around the cabin, but we found nothing. So we torched the cabin to discourage him from coming back. We'll start the search again at first light, but my guess is he's gone."

And Pa was right. The posse combed the woods for several days in a row, while folks in town and the outlying farms held their breath in fear. But there was no sign of Rupp. By the time the sheriff returned to town with his now-useless search warrant, everyone agreed that the vampire calling himself Rupp had fled the county.

Mama made me carry garlic and holy amulets on me whenever I went outside that autumn and winter. But by the time spring rolled around, even she was convinced that the vampire was gone. She and Pa strictly forbade me to go near the burned-out cabin in the woods. Not that they needed to. I still had nightmares about that moment I'd found the dismembered body of the traveling salesman in the bushes and heard Rupp's voice behind me. I probably always would.

Some folks in town say the men overreacted that night. They say Rupp was a sadistic killer, but no vampire. But Josh and I know better. He bought me a silver cross for my last birthday and had it specially blessed by a priest. When he gave it to me, he made me promise that I would wear it around my neck all the days of my life and never take it off. That's a vow I intend to keep!

30

The Lady

"If only . . ." The phrase came frequently to the lips of the good Doctor and his wife. If only they had time and energy. If only they had money. If only they had assistance. But they had none of these things. For themselves, they asked for little, but for their children they wanted everything. It shamed the Doctor and his wife that they had nothing to give their children, not even an education.

The Doctor was severely injured in the Civil War and had walked with a limp since the second battle of Manassas. This injury kept him from doing a full day of physician rounds, and it made his life a misery when he was called out to a birth in the middle of the night. On his dear wife fell the burden of keeping house and home up and running, itself an awesome task. The couple had no money to hire help, since the residents of post-war Virginia could only pay the good Doctor in food and clothing. Without money, they couldn't afford the luxury of hiring a tutor for their intelligent sons or a music teacher for their gifted daughter. And the children—who worked as hard as their parents to make ends meet—were so sleepy at night that

THE LADY

they often fell asleep before the Doctor or his wife could spare time to give them a lesson.

The Doctor and his wife were rehashing the issue of their children's education one evening as a mighty storm raged over the countryside. The Doctor's injured hip ached with the cold and humidity, and he huddled next to the warmth of the fire, too tired to rise and go to bed. As his good wife knitted and fretted beside him, there came a faint knock on the front door.

"Oh no," moaned the wife. "Not tonight. You are too sore and weary to go out, my dear husband."

"You know that I took an oath to answer the summons of those in need," the Doctor replied gently, using both hands to push himself out of the chair. He grabbed his wife's arm for support as he limped toward the door.

The couple opened the door together and staggered backward as wind and rain whipped inside, almost knocking them over. At first, their fire-dazzled eyes perceived nothing but darkness. Then the wife looked down and saw a woman lying in a pathetic, soaking wet heap at their feet. The Doctor picked the woman up and carried her to the fire, while his wife pushed the door shut with much effort against the wind.

The woman was far gone with cold and fatigue. The Doctor dried her off and wrapped her in warm blankets, all the while speculating on who this stranger might be. The Doctor knew every man, woman, and child for nearly fifty miles, but he had never seen this woman before. She was unnaturally pale, as if she spent all of her waking life indoors, and her wrists were red and swollen as if the cuffs of her tight sleeves—now mere rags—had cut off her circulation. The Doctor bound the strange wrist injuries while his wife administered a stimulant.

When the Lady roused at last, her eyes focused first upon the library which lined the walls of the Doctor's small parlor. "Books," she murmured. "Books! It has been so long . . ." She closed her eyes weakly, but there was a smile upon her face.

"Shh," said the wife, smoothing back her tangled hair. "You can read your fill tomorrow. Tonight you must rest."

The Lady fell into a deep sleep, and they put her on the bed in the tiny spare room that the Doctor used as his office. Then they went upstairs to their own room for the night.

The morning after the storm dawned glorious and fair. The Doctor's wife lingered over her milking, enjoying the sights and smells of a world washed clean. As she carried her pails toward the house, she heard an angelic voice singing her favorite song, accompanied by the long-disused parlor piano.

"Sweet Amaryllis, by a spring's sweet side . . ." trilled the lovely soprano. The wife beamed, recognizing her daughter Virginia's voice. But who was playing the piano?

The wife hurried inside just as Virginia's song broke off. A sweet contralto commanded: "Sing the line again with a full breath, Virginia. Don't break the phrase in the middle." The pale Lady spoke from her seat on the piano bench. Her pale hands, ringed by bandages, lay upon the keys.

Seeing the Doctor's wife in the doorway, the Lady added: "Madam, your daughter has great talent and may be one of the Great Singers of the world if she is properly trained."

Opposite her, the Doctor and his two sons stood listening in the door to the kitchen, faces beaming with delight.

"Can you teach her, Lady?" asked the Doctor.

The Lady's eyes traveled from the radiant Virginia to the eager faces of the two boys.

"I can teach them all, Sir," she replied.

And teach them she did, with skill and authority and the simple magic possessed by the greatest teachers which calls forth the very best from the minds under their tutelage. The children soaked in their instruction and studied harder than they ever had before, striving to please the Lady they loved.

The Lady never told the family her name. After the first inquiry, they did not ask again, assuming she had run away from a cruel husband or father and needed a place of refuge. It did not bother them, for she was their Lady, the children's beloved governess, come to the Doctor's family to fulfill their great need.

For five years, the Lady strove mightily to educate the Doctor's family, until both boys had qualified for university and Virginia had learned all she could teach and could sing sweetly in three languages. Early one evening, as a great storm rolled into the valley, the children's governess looked one last time upon her sleeping charges, knowing she had done everything she could to ready them for the wide world. Then she slipped away—as she had first come—during the lashing winds and thunderous rains of the storm.

The Doctor and his family wore themselves to the bone searching for their beloved Lady, to no avail. She was gone as a mist, not to be seen again. "Perhaps she was an angel, sent to minister to us in our time of need," the wife said to her family and friends. "God works in mysterious ways."

Soon the children were grown and flown, the boys to university and Virginia on a classical music tour that spanned three continents. Of all the songs the great singer performed, the best loved was the old Southern ballad called "Sweet

Amaryllis." Virginia wept whenever she sang it, remembering her beloved Lady.

The Doctor had prospered in the years following the disappearance of the Lady. Once his children were grown, he turned more and more to charitable works and the donation of his professional time to those in need. One morning, the Doctor paid a visit to an infamous Asylum for the Insane. The Asylum superintendent herself took him on a tour of the facilities. They walked through the narrow hallways, accompanied for safety by two husky orderlies, discussing public health improvements and the best ways to treat the medically insane.

As the group turned into the corridor that housed the more violent patients, the Doctor heard a sweet contralto voice singing "Sweet Amaryllis." The Doctor stopped abruptly before the barred door from which the voice emerged and asked the matron about the inmate.

"An interesting case," the superintendent said. "She was left upon our doorstep one night many years ago—before my time—bound hand and foot to keep her from committing violence against herself and others. After several years in the Asylum, she broke out of her shackles and vanished, only to reappear five years later and beg to be readmitted. She was afraid she would hurt someone in her madness."

"What is her name?" the Doctor asked.

"We never knew her name. We just call her the Lady. Sometimes the Lady can be very gentle, but in my experience the gentle ones are the worst kind. You never know when they might lash out. Don't you agree, doctor?"

Behind the door, the song broke off abruptly in a sob that broke the good Doctor's heart. "Open this door," he commanded to the orderlies.

The superintendent looked alarmed. "Doctor, be careful. The Lady is extremely dangerous."

As the door swung open, the Doctor saw a familiar pale form standing in the middle of the room. Long chains bound the Lady to the wall. Her wrists, under the shackles, were swollen and red. The wounds were the same as those the Doctor had bandaged five years before. The Lady's eyes were closed, and she swayed as she hummed a few more bars of "Sweet Amaryllis."

"Remove those shackles," the Doctor commanded, stepping briskly toward his former governess.

The Lady's eyes flew open, and the Doctor found himself gazing into pupils glowing red with insane hatred and a lust to kill. He stopped in his tracks, stunned by the evil menace twisting the beloved countenance. In that frozen moment, the Lady sprang to the full length of her chains, her long fingernails clawing at the Doctor's face. He fell to the floor, blood streaming from both eyes, and the Lady laughed maniacally as she stood in triumph over her latest victim.

The husky orderlies leapt into the room and wrestled the Lady down onto the bed while the superintendent dragged the Doctor to safety. But it was too late to save him. The Doctor's eyes were permanently damaged by the Lady's blow. He never saw again.

31

Devil in the Flour Barrel

There was once an old revival preacher by the name of Crabtree who was looking for a place to hold a big-time tent meeting. He searched around till he found some acreage he liked over in Amherst County. It was a lovely grove of trees by a creek that was deep enough for baptizing. Crabtree met with Moreland, the chap who owned the place, to see if the fellow would let him hold a camp meeting on his property. But Moreland was not big on religion. He said "no" mighty quick to the preacher-man's request and sent him on his way.

Crabtree was disheartened by Moreland's hard-hearted attitude. He took a room for the night at the local inn while he prayed over the situation. He was sure the Lord was calling him to hold a revival in that town. But where?

When the innkeeper came to take his supper order, Crabtree told the man that the little wooded area across the street from the tavern might be a fine place to have a prayer meeting. But Mister Beaton, the innkeeper, was as hard-hearted as Moreland. He didn't want religious folks hanging around across the street from the tavern because it would be bad for business.

DEVIL IN THE FLOUR BARREL

Crabtree was still nursing his drink of water and wondering what to do when the innkeeper's pretty wife came out to give him a smile and a refill. Missus Beaton explained that her husband had just left on an overnight trip; she would be serving him for the rest of the evening. The preacher was quite taken with the pretty lass. He perked up and told her all about his idea for a camp meeting. Missus Beaton was sympathetic to his cause and told him it was a shame there wasn't more religion around these parts.

It being a Saturday night, the tavern began filling with local farmers and wayside travelers. Soon the ale was flowing and folks were making jokes that made the preacher's lily-white soul writhe. He was about to return to his bedchamber when Moreland came in with his son, a handsome young chap with a charming way about him.

The sight of the landowner filled the preacher with a righteous rage. Crabtree leapt up suddenly, his chair crashing loudly to the floor, and began preaching revival with fire and vigor. So carried away was he that he climbed right up onto the bar and began urging the sinners in the tavern to repent their wicked ways.

"You need a revival," he cried. "You need to come back to the Lord before your sins carry you straight to hell. Sinner, you are at a fork in the road. One way leads to glory and the other to the pit! Which road will you choose? I can hear the Devil now, flapping his wings at the window of this very tavern!"

The boisterous crowd in the taproom was gaping at him, too astonished by his sudden tirade to speak. Glaring at Moreland, Crabtree roared, "You need a camp meeting, sinners, in the grove down by the creek, where hundreds—nay, thousands—of sinners can repent of their sins and come to the Lord!"

Several of the men stirred in their seats and looked interested in the proposition. But at that moment the front door of the inn burst open and a group of musicians breezed in, calling out greetings and setting up their instruments for a square dance. Crabtree's sermonizing was instantly forgotten.

Chagrined, the preacher slid down off the bar and retreated to a vacant parlor next door to the taproom. It was bare save for a big flour barrel, a sofa, and a deep chair by the empty fireplace. Weary and discouraged, the preacher-man settled into the chair to pray. "Lord, if I'm to hold a revival in this county, you're gonna have to help me find a place," he said with an unhappy sigh.

Just then the door opened and a couple slipped into the room and sat down on the sofa. To Crabtree's surprise, he recognized Missus Beaton and Moreland's young son. They embraced each other passionately, and young Moreland began begging the innkeeper's wife to run away with him. Embarrassed, the preacher wondered whether he should confront the erring young people at once or take them aside individually to chide them for their sins.

As he hesitated, the fiddling in the next room ceased and several voices called out greetings to the innkeeper. On the sofa, young Moreland and Missus Beaton froze in horror. They heard the innkeeper's voice outside the door explaining that his meeting had been canceled so he'd decided to come home.

"Quick," Missus Beaton said to young Moreland. "Hide in the flour barrel! My husband always comes in here to hang up his coat. If he finds you with me, he'll kill us both!"

Young Moreland sprang from the sofa, wrenched the lid from the flour barrel, and scrambled inside. Puffs of flour rose from the barrel, and Missus Beaton thrust the lid down to hide them. Then she turned toward the door and saw Crabtree for the first time. Her pretty mouth fell open in shock, but before she could speak, the parlor door opened and in came her husband. As soon as he saw his wife, his face hardened with suspicion. His eyes swept the room, taking in the flour spilled on the floor. Then he saw the preacher sitting in the chair and blinked in surprise.

Missus Beaton was instantly all smiles as she explained to her husband that she was showing the preacher the parlor, thinking he'd find it more hospitable than the taproom while the square dance was going on. Hearing her voice, several of the regulars at the tavern came over to the parlor door to see what was happening.

Meanwhile, Crabtree was debating with himself. Here was a possible solution to his problem. He could blackmail the elder Moreland into letting him have the camp meeting by promising not to tell the innkeeper about his son's indiscretion. But was it right to conceal a sin to bring about something good? No. No matter how tempting the idea, Crabtree knew it would be wrong. To blackmail the farmer would be as heinous a sin as that which he'd just witnessed. He'd have to confront the sinners immediately, even if it meant losing forever his chance at revival in Amherst County.

The crowd in the doorway was getting bigger by the moment as the preacher rose, squared his shoulders, and declaimed in his best pulpit voice, "This room is *full* of sin!"

The innkeeper rocked back on his heels, startled by the announcement. "What do you mean, preacher?" he asked.

"The Devil himself is right here right now," Crabtree roared, "and I can prove it to you!"

He strode over to the flour barrel and whipped off the cover. Instantly a wild-eyed figure covered in white flour burst forth from the barrel. It leapt onto the parlor floor, its ghastly arms windmilling for balance as it moaned with terror. Then the ghostly figure raced out through a service door past a wide-eyed cook and fled into the night.

The men crowding in the parlor doorway gave shouts of fear and alarm. "A hant! I seen a hant!" screamed the cook from the kitchen.

"It's the ghost of evil and sin!" roared the preacher man. "Repent, ye sinners!"

Several of the taverngoers fell to their knees on the floor to pray as a frantic kitchen worker raced into the room to report that the ghost had just vanished into the woods behind the inn. Crabtree offered up a prayer against evil, and everyone inside the parlor joined in, convinced they had just seen a ghost. A few men swore off drinking on the spot.

Then the preacher-man looked the elder Moreland straight in the eye and said, "I want to thank Mister Moreland for loaning us ten acres of his land to hold a camp meeting. It's a vital step that will keep that ghost from taking on a human form we might recognize."

Crabtree turned slightly to gaze meaningfully at Missus Beaton as he spoke.

Moreland swallowed as he finally realized who had *really* been hiding in the flour barrel. "Twenty acres, preacher," he shouted at once. "Ten acres ain't enough to hold all the prayin' folks we need to banish that there ghost."

Twenty acres! It was more than the preacher had dreamed of. And it had been spoken aloud in front of all these witnesses, so Moreland couldn't back out. God truly worked in mysterious ways!

"Hallelujah! Brothers, did you hear? That's twenty acres of land for our big revival down by the creek," Crabtree roared, making sure that everyone in the parlor got the message loud and clear. Then the preacher-man flung his arms toward heaven and cried: "Praise the Lord!"

And everyone in the parlor shouted "Amen!"

32

Consecration

My thoughts were so troubled that I could not settle myself to sleep that night. Again and again I wrestled with my conscience. The future of my homeland was at stake. Many were the injustices we had suffered at the hands of the king. Great was the taxation he forced upon us to pay for his wars abroad. And yet he was our king. I struggled in my mind, trying to answer one question: Is it lawful for a subject to draw sword against his king?

Many of my friends and colleagues had no hesitation in answering yes. But I had served in the armed forces for his majesty. To turn against the man I had once served was treason, no matter how I looked at it. And yet . . . he had turned against us. The history of the present king of Great Britain was a history of repeated injuries and usurpations. His objective seemed to be the establishment of an absolute tyranny over the American Colonies. When a government becomes destructive, when it fails to honor the rights of its people, did they have the right to abolish it and institute a new government? I didn't know the answer to that question either.

CONSECRATION

I fled from my bed, realizing that I would find no answers here. And my restless tossing and turning was disturbing my good wife. So I went to the stable, saddled my horse, and rode off into the cold winter night. Snow crunched underfoot as I traveled I knew not where, struggling with the issues. I must be clear in my own mind. If I could not find peace within myself, I was useless both to myself and to my country.

My horse walked far that night, going hither and yon until I was on paths completely unknown to me. All the while I wrestled with my conscience. Many of my compatriots felt that the united colonies ought to be free and independent states, absolved from all allegiance to the British Crown. But to overturn a government long established—that could not, must not be done lightly. Of this I was morally certain. Yet when a long train of abuses evinces a design to rule a people by absolute despotism, what then? Was Jefferson right? Was Henry? Was it their duty to throw off such government and provide new guards for their future?

Suddenly I realized I was cold, hungry, and lost. I looked around for a signpost but saw none. However, there was a light through the trees, indicating a dwelling somewhere ahead of me. I could inquire my way from the good people who lived therein. I turned my horse in that direction, and we made our way through untrodden snow up to the long, low dwelling.

Above me, the wind sighed deeply in the treetops. It was very late for the occupants of the house to be up. Or perhaps it was nearing dawn. I could not tell, for the cloudy sky hid the stars.

I dismounted and walked to the front door. I had barely lifted my hand from the first knock when the door swung open and I found myself face to face with a small, round man. He was fully dressed, and he beamed a smile upon me that was almost worshipful. The little man ushered me into his home. Behind him stood two young people, quite probably a son and daughter.

I bowed to them all politely and said, "Friends, I have lost my way. Can you direct me?"

The old man turned brilliant eyes upon me, and the intensity in his face made me uneasy. "You have not lost your way," he said. "You have found it." His voice seemed to ring around the room like the voice of an angel delivering a message from God. "You have been called to a great mission. Kneel at this altar and receive it."

My eyes following his gesture, I saw a small altar on the far side of the room. A cross hung above it, and on either side were portraits, one of the Virgin Mary and the other of John the Baptist raising the newly baptized Son of God out of the waters of the Jordan River.

I did not know what to think. I looked back at the old man, doubt in my eyes. Was he mad? He smiled at the look on my face.

"Nay, lad. I am not mad. The Lord told me of your coming in a dream. Do you doubt me? Then let me tell you why you are out so late on a winter night. Tonight you could not sleep, so disturbed were you for the future of your country. So you mounted your horse and rode out into the countryside to ponder the question that haunts your every waking hour: Is it lawful for a subject to draw sword against his king?"

I gasped and took a step backward. That was exactly the question on my mind. How had he known? I looked from him to his son and daughter and then over to the altar in the corner of the room.

He continued, his voice gentle but firm, "Your horse wandered you knew not where, nor did you care, so tangled were you in your thoughts. And so he brought you finally to this house, where we have been waiting for you to arrive."

"How do you know this?" I asked in amazement. "You said there was a prophecy?"

"Yes, my son," he replied. "The Lord spoke to me in a dream and told me that at the third hour of the morning, the deliverer would present himself to me. A voice said, 'I will send a deliverer to the New World who shall save my people from bondage, as my Son saved them from spiritual death.'"

I gaped at him, his words ringing in my head. A deliverer who shall save my people from bondage . . .

"Be not surprised," the old man said quietly, "but kneel while I anoint thee the deliverer of this land."

My head spinning, I knelt before the altar in the corner and felt the man anoint my forehead with oil. Then he asked, "Do you promise, when the hour shall strike, to take the sword in defense of your country? Do you promise, when you shall see your soldiers suffer for bread and fire, and when the people you have led to victory shall bow before you, to remember that you are but the minister of God in the work of a nation's freedom?"

"The minister of God in the work of a nation's freedom." The words settled around me like a comforting quilt, and the burden of indecision I had been carrying for so long suddenly slipped off my shoulders.

"I so promise," I said, feeling suddenly light and free. And more than that, I felt as though a fire had been lit inside my breast. In that moment, I knew where my destiny lay.

"Then in God's name, I consecrate thee deliverer of this oppressed people. When the time comes, go forth to victory for, as you are faithful, be sure that God will grant it. Wear no crown save the spiritual one granted you by the blessings and honor of a free people."

As he finished speaking, his daughter came forward and placed a wreath of laurel on my head. The old man bid me rise, and his son came forward and carefully buckled a sheathed sword around my waist. Then the prophet spoke a benediction.

Moved beyond words, I drew the sword, kissed the hilt, and laid my free hand upon the Bible on the altar. "I will keep the faith," I said in a choked voice.

Then I turned and went quietly out the front door and mounted my patient horse. I did not ask for directions. Somehow I knew the way home. I turned my horse toward the east and followed the road as the sky lightened slowly from black to gray and then to the pinks and pearly whites of dawn.

My restlessness of the previous night was gone. My question was answered. Was it lawful for a subject to draw sword against his king? In the light of the new dawn, every fiber of my being resonated with one word: "Yes!"

I tucked the laurel wreath into my coat pocket before I rode into the yard. I was not ready yet to talk about the strange experience I'd had in the night. Already it seemed more like a dream than reality, save for the wreath in my pocket and the sword at my side.

Several of the stable attendants came out to greet me and take my horse. I surrendered my faithful steed to their attentions, patting him on the neck and whispering a word of thanks in his ear for carrying me through the long winter night. Then I walked up to the house. The front door was opened immediately and a house servant bowed and said, "Good morning, Mr. Washington."

"Good morning," I replied. And it was.

The Honest Wine Merchant

RICHMOND

When he first set up his winery in the capital city, he had very little custom. But by nature and practice, he was an honest merchant who only sold the best. And those who discovered his wares told others. By word of mouth, his reputation spread throughout the city until all the finest families were purchasing their wine from him.

The honest wine merchant valued his reputation above money. If any customer found a bottle or keg or casket of wine sold in his shop to be less than perfect, he would return their money forthwith. This never happened of course, for he had excellent taste in wine and was an excellent judge of the wines he purchased from sea captains docking their ships in the James River. But knowing that such a policy existed brought comfort to the minds of his customers, and more and more people flocked to his shop.

As the years passed, the honest merchant became friends with a number of rising young men in the city. Whenever a new cask of some very special wine arrived from abroad, the merchant would invite his friends to visit his office above the wine cellars and sample the new vintage with him. It was a very

THE HONEST WINE MERCHANT

popular—and very exclusive—event. Any man receiving such an invitation was the envy of his less-fortunate friends.

One day the merchant received a message that one of the captains he worked with had docked with a very special pipe of wine. Immediately he sent his servant out with special invitations to his friends while another fetched the pipe—a 140-gallon cask of wine—from the ship. It was a very rare Burgundy, laid down a hundred years ago. Twice around Cape Horn had the captain carried this cask before it came to rest with the honest wine merchant.

A few hours after the cask arrived in the shop, the office of the wine merchant was packed with eager young men. The honest merchant handed around glasses filled with the Burgundy, and the city's young doctor raised his glass and offered a toast to such a rare wine and a fine host.

"To your health," the other young men echoed, and everyone drank deeply of the fine vintage.

As he emptied his glass, the young doctor became aware of an itch on his upper lip, as though some foreign object were clinging to his mustache. Reaching up with his fine linen handkerchief, he plucked a long golden hair from his upper lip. The young doctor blinked in astonishment. Where had the hair come from? Could it have been in the wine?

As he hastily put down his wine glass, he realized that the young colonel beside him was likewise gazing in horror at something in his handkerchief. He motioned to his friend, and they turned aside into a corner. Upon seeing a second golden hair in the possession of the young doctor, the colonel swallowed hastily and put his own glass down.

"We have to tell the merchant," he whispered to the doctor.

The young doctor nodded reluctantly. "But not now. We do not want to shame him in front of his customers. He could lose his business over this if it were discovered."

The two men lingered after the others had departed amidst laughter and high spirits. When they were alone with their friend, they showed the wine merchant the long golden hairs that each had found in his wine. The merchant's eyes widened in horror. In his entire professional career, nothing like this had ever before marred his purchases.

"My friends! I am aghast," he cried. "Come. We must examine this pipe of Burgundy at once to see what has caused such a thing to happen."

The wine merchant and his two friends descended into the cryptlike cellars below the shop, following the merchant's personal man-servant, who carried two torches to light their way. They were surrounded by towering casks of vintage wine, and the flicker of the torchlight cast shadows into all the corners and spaces between the massive casks.

About halfway down one corridor stood the massive cask of Burgundy, newly arrived from Europe after two trips around Cape Horn. The young doctor sighed at such a waste of good Burgundy, but it could not be helped. Rolling up their sleeves, the two young men helped their friend decant the expensive vintage. They removed the bung from the bottom half of the pipe and watched the wine pulsing out into the overflow barrel below it.

Flowing in a ruby stream, the wine gleamed in the flickering light of the torches. The eyes of all four men watched intently, not sure what they might see. When the overflow barrel was full, they replaced it with another. This continued until the flow of wine from the pipe decreased in volume, and the original swish and gurgle changed to a murmur and a sigh.

And then, from the mouth of the pipe came a coil of long golden tresses, shimmering among the red wine. It fell into the overflow bucket and floated there as the men stared in horror.

"Mein Gott," gasped the wine merchant. "How could such a thing have gotten into the Burgundy?"

The young doctor ordered the servant to take a hatchet and open the top of the pipe. But the man was cowering in a corner, unable to take his eyes off the long, golden tresses floating on a sea of Burgundy. Finally the young colonel grabbed the hatchet and climbed the small ladder. With a couple of mighty blows, he managed to open the pipe. Taking a torch from the merchant, he thrust it into the opening—and froze, a look of utter horror twisting his face. He gasped and began trembling so hard that the doctor leapt forward to steady his legs, lest he fall and injure himself.

"What is it, man?" he cried, both impatient to know the truth and terrified of whatever had transformed the brave young colonel into a quivering mass of fear.

The colonel tried to speak but couldn't get a word past the lump in his throat. Finally he slid down the ladder and collapsed onto the floor, his legs unable to hold him. The young doctor took his place on the ladder, gazed for one terrible moment, and then gave way to the honest merchant.

Curled up on the bottom of the pipe was the white, unclothed figure of a woman. She was beautiful among the dregs of the Burgundy; her long hair wrapping about her body like a golden curtain. Her mouth, palms, and ears were stained a deep reddish-pink from the Burgundy in which her body had lain for—if the stamp of the maker were true—a hundred years.

The young doctor stood with his head against the wood of the pipe, his stomach lurching. They had drunk the wine, and all the time she was in there . . . The thought sent him running into the shadows to be sick in a corner. Finally pulling himself together—he was a doctor, after all—he once again climbed the ladder to examine the corpse inside. She was a young girl, he announced to his companions. There was no sign of physical violence—no obvious blows to the head or injuries marring her wine-stained skin.

"What happened?" the colonel asked quietly from his seat on the floor. "How did she get in there?"

No one could answer his question. Perhaps a spurned lover had seen her working alone at the wine press and had thrust her into the pipe while it was being filled? They would never know.

To protect the reputation and business of the honest wine merchant, the young doctor and the colonel wrapped up the girl's body and carried it to an old graveyard under cover of darkness to bury her in an unmarked tomb in a land far from her home.

To the end of their days, the doctor and the colonel both longed for and were sickened by the taste of Burgundy. And the sight of a young girl with long golden tresses always sent a shiver up their spines.

The Seventh Window

CHARLOTTESVILLE

Veronica hated her confined life. Her domineering father would not let her go to dances or introduce her into society. After the death of her mother, the dark-haired beauty became a virtual prisoner in her own home, attending to her father's every whim and listening silently to his nightly tantrums. Veronica's life was unbearable, and she desperately sought escape from the lovely mansion that was her prison.

Escape came in the autumn of 1890, when the mysterious Mr. Rutherford began calling on Veronica after her father had retired to his rooms for the evening. Heretofore, she had only heard rumors about the rich, elderly miser. The people in town said he lived alone in a decrepit old mansion on the far side of town with only one deaf servant to cook his meals and tend to his meager needs. Mr. Rutherford never came to town for any reason. His deaf servant did all his banking and shopping for him.

Once a month a mysterious shipment of unlabeled boxes arrived at the train station for the rich miser. The delivery man was instructed to take the shipment to the mansion and leave the large, heavy boxes on the stoop. The mansion door never

THE SEVENTH WINDOW

opened while the delivery man was on the grounds. Folks in town frequently debated what those boxes might contain, but no one was invited into the mansion to find out.

On his first visit, Mr. Rutherford stayed for a half hour and made small talk with Veronica in the approved society fashion. He was a tall, white-haired gentleman with a cultured voice and hard black eyes. His dark suit had a faintly chemical smell about it that Veronica found repellent. But he was the only suitor who dared brave her father's wrath, so what choice did she have?

Once a week for the next two months, Mr. Rutherford paid court to the lovely eighteen-year-old. The blue-eyed, dark-haired beauty used every wile at her disposal to attract the old man, so desperate was she for escape. *Please, God, let him propose,* she prayed each night. And propose he did, to her intense relief.

Veronica's father was furious when he learned of her clandestine courtship. He threw her bags onto the lawn and locked the door behind her when her betrothed arrived to take her to their town hall wedding. Disowned forever, Veronica resolved to forget her old life as her bridegroom drove her away from her former home.

Veronica's new resolve was shaken when she caught her first glimpse of the decrepit old Rutherford mansion on the far side of town. It was surrounded by a ruined hulk of a garden and bizarrely segmented cracked brick walkways. Detritus was piled so high against the double front doors that the newlyweds were forced to enter the mansion through the portal at the back.

Rutherford disappeared into the depths of the mansion without a word, leaving Veronica in the ruined back hallway with the elderly deaf maidservant. Veronica almost choked on the horrible chemical smell that pervaded the whole house. The stale dusty air made her sneeze, and her lovely blue eyes watered unattractively as she followed the maidservant through the worn-out hallway. They climbed a magnificent, cobweb-encrusted staircase and entered a large bedroom on the second floor.

The servant dropped Veronica's bag beside the fireplace and withdrew, leaving the bereft bride staring at the tattered tapestries, the worn-out chair coverings, and the faded quilt on the large canopy bed that rose like a bier in the center of the room.

When Veronica pulled aside the tattered bed curtains, she was suddenly enveloped by tiny white moths that fluttered sickeningly around her. She gasped and flailed at the creatures, their tiny wings brushing her face and neck like grasping fingers. The moths vanished as suddenly as they had appeared, and Veronica pressed a hand to her pounding heart, the chemical smell strong in her nostrils.

All at once, Veronica's eyes focused on the large, faded bed she shortly would be sharing with her new husband. The idea made her stomach roil, and she lunged for the shutters that covered the window, longing for fresh air. But the window catch was rusted shut, and she could not open it.

Defeated, Veronica turned back into the room. Her eye was caught suddenly by a large portrait hanging above the fireplace. A lovely blonde bride leaned her elbow against a marble pillar, her lovely cheek resting on her hand. Her bridal veil cascaded around her intricately arranged hair, and a marvelous necklace of rubies enwreathed her smooth neck. Her free hand lay on the head of a large French poodle. Tiny white slippers peeped out from underneath her magnificent white dress. Veronica stared entranced at the portrait and then glanced ruefully down at her own wedding suit of conservative blue and gray.

At that moment, a pair of folding doors on the far side of the room slid open. Veronica realized with a start that her bedroom must adjoin that of Rutherford, for he stood observing her from the doorway. "If you would be so good as to join me?" he said politely. "Supper is served."

Veronica swallowed and nodded. She passed through the folding doors and looked apprehensively around her husband's apartment. Rutherford's room was larger than hers. It was quickly apparent that he spent much of his time there, for the room was a combination study and bedroom. Books lined two walls, and against the third wall stood a small dining table and a hideous iron stove. The bed with its dusty spread and sagging springs was relegated to a far corner, as if it was of small importance.

The newlyweds sat in silence while the deaf maidservant served a mouthwatering meal. Veronica broke the silence to inquire about the fancy portrait above her fireplace.

"She was my first wife," Rutherford said abruptly, in a tone that brooked no further questions. Veronica gulped and thereafter stayed silent. When the meal was done, Rutherford stood politely and motioned for Veronica to go to her room.

Veronica departed with racing heart, aware that it was her wedding night and that she had married a man she did not love. The faintly sweet chemical smell assaulted her nostrils afresh as she entered her apartment. The folding doors closed behind her, and bile rose suddenly in her throat. Stomach churning, she was overwhelmed by a desire for fresh air. Veronica bolted for the hallway and ran down the stairs and through the decrepit hall to the back door.

Veronica's hand was on the knob when the elderly maidservant appeared from nowhere and caught hold of her arm in a gentle but ruthless grip. Veronica stared at the blank-faced woman in sudden fear, and then she became aware of a clap of thunder overhead and the pounding of rain against the roof of the mansion. Wind shook the house from top to bottom as the maidservant withdrew, leaving Veronica alone in the storm-beleaguered hallway.

Resigned to her fate, Veronica went upstairs and put on her nightgown. She sat by the fire to wait for the appearance of her new husband, breathing deeply of the dusty, stifling air inside the worn-out room. Slowly her dark lashes sank against her cheeks, and she fell into a deep sleep.

In the early hours of the morning, Rutherford came silently through the folding doors carrying a small flashlight and a tape measure. He regarded his sleeping bride thoughtfully as she lay in the chair by the flickering fire. Then he looked up at the portrait above the fireplace. He seemed to be making some kind of mental comparison between his former bride and the new one. Then he took the tape and began measuring his sleeping bride from head to hips, from hip to knee, from knee to toe. Length of arm. Length of feet. Length of fingers. Length of neck. He fingered a dark tress of hair as if assessing its texture. So light was his touch that Veronica never awoke. Measurements completed, Rutherford withdrew as silently as he had arrived.

Veronica woke the next morning when the servant arrived with breakfast. She begged the maid to open the window shutters to let in the fresh air. The deaf woman went next door to consult with her master and then silently returned to open the shutters. A moment later, Rutherford opened the folding doors. Veronica's heart thudded in belated panic. She had slept through her wedding night, and now her hour of wifely reckoning was upon her. But Rutherford merely inquired after her sleep and asked her to join him for lunch. Veronica's panic changed to puzzlement. It seemed her elderly husband did not wish a physical relationship with his new wife.

And so it proved in the days that followed. Veronica took meals with her elderly husband, who then withdrew to his own pursuits, leaving her alone to read or sew. She spent a good bit of her first week wandering through the decrepit mansion. On the morning after her wedding, Veronica explored the dusty, unfurnished rooms with shuttered windows on the first floor. She found a stack of paintings in a corner covered by a dusty sheet, but none were as fine as the bridal portrait in her bedroom. The next day she explored the unoccupied bedrooms on the second floor, but there was little to interest her, and she soon grew bored and withdrew to her apartment to read.

On her third day, Veronica investigated the third floor. As she turned the corner of the third-floor landing, she stepped into a sunbeam filled with hundreds and hundreds of white moths. They fluttered around her, suffocating her just as they had the first night she arrived. Veronica shrieked and batted at them, finally covering her head with her arms and fleeing upward to get away.

As Veronica reached the top step, dry wings brushed her dark hair. Looking up, she saw a stuffed seagull hanging from a wire at the top of the stair. When she looked down the hallway, hundreds of glass eyes stared at her from every nook and cranny along its length. A stuffed fox sniffed the air. A red-jacketed monkey sat on a chair. An owl perched on a log. A cat lounged on a cushion.

Everywhere Veronica looked, dead animals glared back at her. It appeared her new husband had a mania for taxidermy. Well, at least this explained the mysterious shipments that came each month on the train. Rutherford was obviously collecting dead animals to stuff. It was a revolting obsession, but there was nothing mysterious about it. At least it explained the moths.

As the weeks passed, Veronica realized that she had replaced one form of captivity with another. True, her new husband did not scream at her. But she had no more freedom of thought and movement now than she had with her autocratic father. Less, even, for she was rarely allowed to walk in the weed-choked garden. She spent her days reading books, wandering alone through the rooms of the mansion, and eating rich meals because her husband thought she needed fattening up.

The maidservant spoke not a word to her new mistress, tending silently to her needs and appearing unexpectedly whenever Veronica wandered too close to her husband's taxidermy workshop. Although Rutherford never forbade her from going up to the third floor, Veronica sensed that her husband and his maidservant did not want her roaming there.

As lonely month followed lonely month, Veronica realized she must escape her constricted life or go insane. She wanted to be free of the elderly miser who ignored her, free of this horror house with its dead animals and moths and dust, free of the maid who was more a keeper than a servant. But Veronica had no way of effecting her escape. The servant did all the shopping, so Veronica had no money. She was never allowed to visit the town. And where could she go if she ran away? Her father would not take her back, and she had no other family.

One evening, as Veronica sat sewing by the fire, futilely running escape options through her anxious mind, her eye fell on the bride's portrait above the fireplace. She stared at the rubies adorning the throat of Rutherford's first wife and realized that those rubies must be someplace in this house. The miserly Rutherford would not have disposed of something so valuable. If she found those rubies, Veronica could go far away and make a new life for herself.

From that moment, Veronica began searching the mansion room by room for the rubies. She would send the maidservant on long errands and then tap on the walls, look under furniture, and search in and around the stuffed animals that filled the third-floor rooms. Veronica hated those animals, so full of dust and chemical smells. They felt so dead when she touched them, preserved for all eternity in a ghastly resurrection that felt beyond redemption. But she touched them anyway, for it occurred to her that a stuffed animal might make a good hiding place for the rubies.

One evening, when the maidservant was sent on an errand for her master, Veronica slipped into Rutherford's taxidermy workshop to search for the rubies and saw that Rutherford was working on a new project. The upper portion of a wax head sat on the workbench, its forehead and dark-lashed eyes already in place. The dark blue glass eyes struck a deep, negative chord in Veronica. A shiver ran down her spine as she gazed into the glass eyes, trying to recall where she'd seen them.

The clock struck in the hallway, and she realized she was wasting precious time. The maidservant would return shortly.

This might be Veronica's only chance to search the workshop. She turned her back on the model and hurriedly searched the room, racing away at the last minute when she heard the back door slam as the maidservant returned to the mansion.

Later that evening, Veronica was taking a rare stroll through the ruined garden when she was struck by an oddity in the construction of the mansion's third floor. In her explorations, she had discovered three big rooms on each side of the third-floor hallway. Each room had two shuttered windows. Three times two made six windows, which were cut into the north and south sides of the mansion. So why were there *seven* shuttered windows on the south side? Veronica counted the third-floor windows several times, and each time she came up with an extra window. Veronica's heart pounded with excitement as she realized that the seventh window must be inside a secret room behind her husband's workshop. And therein, she was suddenly sure, she would find the rubies.

Over the next few weeks, Veronica slipped to the third floor whenever she could to search for the hidden room. She tapped the walls and pressed the molding and inspected every inch of the hallway and workshop. She was about to give up in despair when her questing fingers found a flexible place in the molding at the far end of the third-floor hallway. When she pressed it, a panel slid aside, revealing a large metal door with a combination lock. Hearing footsteps on the staircase, she hastily pressed the molding again and the door slid shut. She hurried to the sniffing fox and stood inspecting it as the suspicious maidservant entered the hall and beckoned to Veronica.

That night, Rutherford called for wine to be served with dinner. They never drank wine, and Veronica eyed its appearance with suspicion.

"Do you know what today is?" her husband asked in an unusually jovial tone. Veronica shook her head. "My dear, it is our anniversary," Rutherford said. "We should drink to our happy union." His eyes were bright with anticipation as he poured red wine into her glass and then fixed himself a tonic and gin. "To us," he said, raising his glass.

Then Rutherford's left arm jerked and the glass fell out of his hand, shattering on the floor as he clutched at his arm. A moment later, he toppled over, dead of a heart attack. Veronica leapt to his side, but it was too late. She stared at his lifeless open eyes, so much like those of his stuffed creatures. Then Veronica called for the maidservant and sent her to summon the doctor. In the hubbub that followed, the nuptial glass of wine stood forgotten until the maidservant found it the next morning and poured it out.

It wasn't until her husband's body was carried away that Veronica realized she no longer needed the rubies. She was a rich widow, and the whole estate was hers to do with as she pleased.

After the funeral, Veronica pensioned off the maidservant handsomely for her years of service and sent her away. Then she put the house up for sale and prepared to move to Richmond to start a new life far away from the old.

While cleaning out her husband's rooms, Veronica found a lock combination hidden inside an old-fashioned pocket watch: "Twenty-four left, five right, sixteen left, nine right." It was then that Veronica remembered the secret door and the missing rubies. She had been so busy with the paperwork and her husband's funeral that she'd forgotten them completely.

Overwhelmed by a sudden desire to find those amazing rubies and take them to Richmond as a reward for her year of misery, Veronica went to the third floor and entered the combination into the lock on the secret door. When she opened the door, Veronica was overwhelmed by the chemical smell in the room. It was even stronger than the smell from her dead husband's workshop. No light came through the shuttered seventh window, so Veronica fetched a lantern from her husband's workshop.

As she reentered the secret room, Veronica gasped in astonishment. The lantern illuminated a life-size replica of the bride's portrait from her room. It was a magnificent painting, more finely detailed than the smaller portrait. Gradually, Veronica's wonder turned to unease. Something wasn't right about the picture. A shudder crept across her skin, and cold beads of sweat formed on her arms and neck when she realized that the scene in front of her was three-dimensional. A shadow flickered underneath the white French poodle, and the light glittered off the rubies at the bride's throat. Veronica swallowed dryly and reached out her hand. Her fingers touched glass.

Horror overwhelmed the new widow as she realized what she beheld. Mr. Rutherford's mania for taxidermy had driven him over the edge of sanity. Here, preserved in chemicals and glass, was the murdered body of his first wife.

A memory flashed before Veronica's inner eye. Once more she saw the partially completed wax head with the dark-lashed blue eyes, and she realized those blue eyes were hers. "No!" Veronica screamed, lashing out blindly with the lantern as she envisioned her own body preserved inside the life-size glass box. The sharp edge of her lantern struck the case, and the glass shattered inward, coating the bride and the poodle inside the box. As fresh air hit the corpse, the wedding gown crumbled to dust, leaving a bare skeleton seated beside the marble column. The sparkling red rubies around her throat were the same shade as the poisoned wine Rutherford had poured into Veronica's glass on the night of their anniversary.

Resources

Alan, Ian. *Virginia Ghosts: They Are Among Us.* Raleigh, NC: Sweetwater Press, 2005.

Asfar, Daniel. *Ghost Stories of Virginia.* Auburn, WA: Lone Pine Publishing, Inc., 2006.

_____. *Haunted Battlefields.* Edmonton, AB: Ghost House Books, 2004.

Asfar, Daniel, and Edrick Thay. *Ghost Stories of America.* Edmonton, AB: Ghost House Books, 2001.

_____. *Ghost Stories of the Civil War.* Edmonton, AB: Ghost House Books, 2003.

Bahr, Jeff, Troy Taylor, and Loren Coleman. *Weird Virginia.* New York: Sterling Publishing Co., Inc., 2007.

Barden, Thomas E. *Virginia Folk Legends.* Charlottesville, VA: University Press of Virginia, 1991.

Battle, Kemp P. *Great American Folklore.* New York: Doubleday & Company, Inc., 1986.

Behrend, Jackie Eileen. *The Hauntings of Williamsburg, Yorktown, and Jamestown.* Winston-Salem, NC: John F. Blair, Publisher, 2006.

Botkin, B. A. (ed.). *A Treasury of American Folklore.* New York: Crown, 1944.

Boyle, Virginia Frazer. *Devil Tales: Black Americana Folk-Lore.* New York: Harper & Brothers Publishers, 1900.

Brewer, J. Mason. *American Negro Folklore.* Chicago: Quadrangle Books, 1972.

Brunvand, Jan Harold. *The Choking Doberman and Other Urban Legends.* New York: W. W. Norton, 1984.

_____. *The Vanishing Hitchhiker.* New York: W. W. Norton, 1981.

Cardin, Rachael. *Dark stories and gruesome murders: An investigation into the legend of Crawford Road.* WTKR.com. Accessed on 5/8/2022 at https://www.wtkr.com/2018/11/14/dark-stories-

and-gruesome-murders-an-investigation-into-the-legend-of-crawford-road/.

Caperton, Helena Lefroy. *Legends of Virginia*. Richmond, VA: Garrett & Massie, Inc., 1950.

Coffin, Tristram P., and Hennig Cohen (eds.). *Folklore in America*. New York: Doubleday & AMP, 1966.

_____. *Folklore from the Working Folk of America*. New York: Doubleday, 1973.

Cohen, Daniel, and Susan Cohen. *Hauntings & Horrors*. New York: Dutton Children's Books, 2002.

Coleman, Christopher K. *Ghosts and Haunts of the Civil War*. Nashville, TN: Rutledge Hill Press, 1999.

Crawford Road. Colonialghosts.com. Accessed on 5/8/2022 at https://colonialghosts.com/crawford-road/.

Dorson, R. M. *America in Legend*. New York: Pantheon Books, 1973.

Downer, Deborah L. *Classic American Ghost Stories*. Little Rock, AR: August House Publishers, Inc.

Editors of Life. *The Life Treasury of American Folklore*. New York: Time Inc., 1961.

Erdoes, Richard, and Alfonso Ortiz. *American Indian Myths and Legends*. New York: Pantheon Books, 1984.

Fearing, Sarah. *Behind the grim legacy of Crawford Road*. WYDaily. com. Accessed on 5/8/2022 at https://wydaily.com/news/local/2018/03/19/behind-the-grim-legacy-of-crawford-road/.

Flanagan, J. T., and A. P. Hudson. *The American Folk Reader*. New York: A. S. Barnes & Co., 1958.

Harris, Andrew. *Ghost hunters investigate legend of Crawford Road Bridge*. WYDaily.com. Accessed on 5/8/2022 at https://wydaily.com/news/local/2018/03/19/behind-the-grim-legacy-of-crawford-road/.

Juliano, Dave, and Tina Carlson. *Haunted Places in Virginia*. TheShadowlands.net. Accessed 10/1/2009 at http://theshadowlands.net/places/virginia.htm.

Kinney, Pamela K. *Haunted Virginia: Legends, Myths & True Tales.* Atglen, PA: Schiffer Publishing Ltd., 2009.

Leach, M. *The Rainbow Book of American Folk Tales and Legends.* New York: The World Publishing Co., 1958.

Lee, Marguerite Dupont. *Virginia Ghosts.* Berryville, VA: Virginia Book Company, 1966.

Leeming, David, and Jake Pagey. *Myths, Legends & Folktales of America.* New York: Oxford University Press, 1999.

Mott, A. S. *Ghost Stories of America,* Vol. 2. Edmonton, AB: Ghost House Books, 2003.

Norman, Michael, and Beth Scott. *Historic Haunted America.* New York: Tor Books, 1995.

Peck, Catherine (ed.). *A Treasury of North American Folk Tales.* New York: W. W. Norton, 1998.

Percy, Alfred. *The Devil in the Old Dominion.* Madison Heights, VA: Percy Press, 1965.

Polley, J. (ed.). *American Folklore and Legend.* New York: Reader's Digest Association, 1978.

Reevy, Tony. *Ghost Train!* Lynchburg, VA: TLC Publishing, 1998.

Rule, Leslie. *Coast to Coast Ghosts.* Kansas City, KS: Andrews McMeel Publishing, 2001.

Schlosser, S. E. *Vision of War.* New York: Americanfolklore.net, 2009. Accessed 10/21/2009 at http://americanfolklore.net/folklore/2009/11/the_vision.html.

Schwartz, Alvin. *Scary Stories to Tell in the Dark.* New York: Harper Collins, 1981.

Skinner, Charles M. *American Myths and Legends,* Vol. 1. Philadelphia: J. B. Lippincott, 1903.

_____. *Myths and Legends of Our Own Land,* Vol. 1 & 2. Philadelphia: J. B. Lippincott, 1896.

Spence, Lewis. *North American Indians: Myths and Legends Series.* London: Bracken Books, 1985.

Taylor, L. B. Jr. *The Ghosts of Charlottesville and Lynchburg and Nearby Environs.* Williamsburg, VA: Virginia Ghosts, 1992.

_____. *The Ghosts of Virginia,* Vol I–XIII. Lynchburg, VA: Progress Printing, 1993–2008.

_____. *The Ghosts of Tidewater and Nearby Environs.* Williamsburg, VA: Virginia Ghosts, 1990.

_____. *The Ghosts of Williamsburg and Nearby Environs.* Williamsburg, VA: Virginia Ghosts, 1983.

_____. *The Ghosts of Williamsburg,* Vol. II. Williamsburg, VA: Virginia Ghosts, 1999.

_____. *Haunted Virginia.* Mechanicsburg, PA: Stackpole Books, 2009.

Thay, Edrick. *Ghost Stories of the Old South.* Edmonton, AB: Ghost House Books, 2003.

Varhola, Michael J. *Ghosthunting Virginia.* Cincinnati, OH: Clerisy Press, 2008.

Warmuth, Donna Akers. *Legends, Stories and Ghostly Tales.* Boone, NC: Laurel Publishing, 2005.

Zeitlin, Steven J., Amy J. Kotkin, and Holly Cutting Baker. *A Celebration of American Family Folklore.* New York: Pantheon Books, 1982.

About the Author

S. E. Schlosser has been telling stories since she was a child, when games of "let's pretend" quickly built themselves into full-length tales acted out with friends. A graduate of Houghton College, the Institute of Children's Literature, and Rutgers University, she created and maintains the award-winning Web site Americanfolklore.net, where she shares a wealth of stories from all fifty states, some dating back to the origins of America. Sandy spends much of her time answering questions from visitors to the site. Many of her favorite e-mails come from other folklorists who delight in practicing the old tradition of who can tell the tallest tale.

About the Illustrator

Artist **Paul G. Hoffman** trained in painting and printmaking, with his first extensive illustration work on assignment in Egypt, drawing ancient wall reliefs for the University of Chicago. His work graces books of many genres—children's titles, textbooks, short story collections, natural history volumes, and numerous cookbooks. For *Spooky Virginia,* he employed a scratchboard technique and an active imagination.